Leading a support group

Leading a support group

A practical guide

Keith Nichols and John Jenkinson

Open University Press

Open University Press
McGraw-Hill Education
McGraw-hill House
Shoppenhangers Road
Maidenhead
Berkshire
England
SL6 2QL

email: enquiries@openup.co.uk
world wide web: www.openup.co.uk

and Two Penn Plaza, New York, NY 10121–2289, USA

First published 2006

A catalogue record of this book is available from the British Library

ISBN 10: 0335 215 696 (pb) 0335 215 70 X (hb)
      13: 9780 335 215690 (pb) 9780 335 215706 (hb)

Library of Congress Cataloging-in-Publication Data
CIP data applied for

Typeset by YHT Ltd, London
Printed in Poland by OZ Graf. S.A.
www.polskabook.pl

Contents

Introduction

Thirty years ago the thought of joining 'a group' was heavily laden with excitement and mystery. The excesses of the encounter and personal growth group movements in America had been captured and spread by film and literature. Various myths had arisen that depicted groups as dangerous places, akin to emotional minefields of a highly destructive potential. In such settings, it seemed, one would either be led to make intimate confessions (later regretted) or be drawn into great sexual licentiousness where clothes came off and morals were set aside with joyous abandonment. Groups were, therefore, for the adventurous and uninhibited. In reality, most of the work involved in the development of group technique was not in the least disreputable. In fact, participants searching for excitement in groups would quite often be disappointed and deflated.

How are groups viewed today? This is not a question with a snappy answer. We would need a formal survey of opinion in order to give exact and reliable information. However, it is clear that group technique has shifted to a position in which it is seen as a serious and, at times, powerful means of education, support and therapy. Indeed, even modern government seems unable to get by without focus groups, a derivative of the group approach. There are now hundreds of texts dealing with one aspect or another of group work and respected academic journals dealing with the group approach have been introduced. This turn to respectability can be traced back to the literature of the 1980s. For example, Aveline and Dryden (1988) edited a collection of papers which served to illustrate the range of applications of group technique in the caring professions and the extent to which group work had already become accepted as a standard option for the caring professions. Since then, this trend has continued. There has also been a parallel increase in the use of various types of group technique in industry and commerce generally where it has been found to be helpful in training and motivational programmes. Overall, then, it is safe to say that group work is now accepted and is here to stay.

Leading a Support Group is not, we must emphasize, just another book about groups. It arises out of another aspect of current attitudes towards groups which might best be described as the burden of lack of confidence. In short, many people who would be quite capable of setting up and running a support group hold back from doing so because they lack the confidence. Often this is in circumstances where a support group is very much needed. A recent incident illustrates this well. Several years ago one of the authors was engaged in a conversation with the nursing sister of a specialist burns unit. The situation was that she wanted to improve the range of support offered in her unit to the team of nurses under her management. Her view was that the nurses were working under considerable and increasing strain. She had been considering the possibility of a support group for her nursing staff. However, no one in her unit had received any training to lead a staff support group, there was no funding to pay for an outside group leader and she did not feel that she could call upon already overburdened psychologist colleagues to run a weekly group for them. As a result, there was no support group and no improved support. The problem was not uncommon. The nursing sister, not unreasonably, worried that leading a support group required some special skills and knowledge that she and her colleagues lacked. Thus, it seemed, if one of them were to risk taking on the leadership of a unit group they could end up floundering in less than helpful confusion. The sense was that, in such circumstances, a support group could turn out to be a futile waste of time and a generally negative experience because nobody really knew what to do. This was an understandable but, in our view, unnecessary lack of confidence. In this book we hope to show that it would have been possible for one of the nurses to have begun a support group, assuming that she had the basic information and the approach to the venture that we are planning to pass on to you in the following pages.

Some may view this as a contentious issue but, as a result of having spent a significant portion of our lives to date working in groups, we both feel confident in our belief that sufficient information and 'know-how' can be imparted in written form to enable, say, people in the caring professions, organizers of self-help movements or those in some kind of personnel work, to set up and run a basic support group. Such a position does, it has to be emphasized, assume that whoever is involved is sensitive to human emotions and is capable of learning from experience in a flexible and, to some extent, independent way. Furthermore, we must be clear that we are referring specifically to support groups, as distinct from therapy groups and personal learning or personal growth groups.

We have given some early space in this book to the task of showing why support is so useful to people in any kind of stress or distress and why this support is often best delivered with a group approach. It should be said that we regard self-care as an essential part of the professional *duties* of anyone whose role is known to have a significant degree of stress. General practitioners, young hospital doctors, counsellors, nurses or other health-care professionals in emotionally demanding work, social workers, teachers, dentists, and certain types of management are just a few of the professions which well-conducted research has revealed to be high in the stress league. Without adequate attention to self-care through the medium of support,

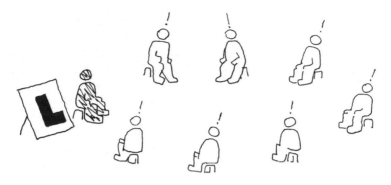

Figure 1 Learning to set up and run a basic support group

people in such professions risk the eventual destructive effects of stress or, alternatively, the more insidious effect of burn-out. The result of this is that professional people are much less efficient in their work, they suffer long periods of illness, or even are lost to their profession because of withdrawal from work entirely. A support group is an excellent means to combat these problems. Although in no way sufficient in itself (effective stress management and individual self-care techniques are also very important), a well-run support group will make an important contribution to the well-being of staff in many and various settings.

Similarly, stressful experiences or demands in life can place people in general under tremendous physical or emotional load. The range involved is daunting; disfiguring or disabling illness and injury, the care-giving role with the seriously ill, elderly or handicapped, traumatic stress experiences, personal struggles in education, career development, marriage and divorce, bereavement, and so on. It is clear from expanding research into the effects of support that people struggling in such stressful and demanding circumstances do fare better both physically and psychologically if they have a good basis of support (see Chapter 1). As we illustrate by means of various examples throughout the book, the support group is ideal as a means of assisting and providing such support for so many differing types of problem.

Overview of the book

Our first task has been to make a reasoned and expanded case for the importance of psychological support to health and well-being in general. We then consolidate our views on the use of the support group format as an efficient means of providing this all-important support in a multiplicity of differing settings. To complement this, there follows a wider assessment of the value of group work and the group experience – with an analysis of the strengths and weaknesses of the approach. Having made these points concerning the usefulness of groups Chapter 2 brings it all to life with several extended examples of support groups in action. Thence we turn to our main task, namely, to teach the basic principles and practicalities of leading a support group. As we have worked on the task we have focused on what we believe to be the needs of a variety of people who share a common situation. Rather like the nursing sister in the example above, they will be faced with a situation in which it is obvious that a support group would be useful, or at least should be given a try. However, they are not at all sure how to go about running a group and consequently lack the confidence to take further steps. We do not offer 'groups by numbers' but have tried to construct a book which, for you, the reader, is rather like having a tutor present in the room explaining essential points and strategies. Thus, as we develop the fantasy of being in a room talking to you, we often write in a conversational style. Throughout the book there is a clear and consistent message: 'You can learn to lead a support group as you go along but, while there is no tablet of stone on which exact rules are set out, a broad set of principles and a broad general track that is clearly explained in the book should be followed. Leading a group should be approached with a reasonable degree of caution and, ideally, someone who has experience as a leader should be sought in order to give supervision and back-up.'

Before a group actually begins, there is much to be done both in the preparation of the leader, in the preparation of the group members and in working out the 'contract' by which the group will run. These three issues are dealt with in turn in Chapters 3, 4 and 5. Chapter 5 also gives guidance on the practical aspects of setting up a group (where, how often, how many members, etc.) and takes you to the point of having conducted your first meeting.

Chapter 6 focuses on the task of giving guidelines for leadership during the ensuing life of a group. In so doing we have remained eclectic in approach, which is to say that no particular named style of group work is favoured and no particular theoretical position is taken. Other than our basic assumptions concerning the value and positive impact of support work in groups, our position is atheoretical, with a practical, caring, common-sense approach given priority over any leaning towards a particular theoretical system. There is, of course, a considerable body of theory relating to therapy and personal training groups. However, these various theories and approaches to group work compete with each other in a manner that does not allow easy resolution and, for someone attempting to run a basic support group, have little direct relevance, in our view. Thus we do not include a structured review of rival systems of theory and technique such as transactional analysis, gestalt group technique, psychodrama, group analysis, and so on. Plenty of texts exist which do present such theory (e.g. Patterson 1986). However, as a person becomes more experienced and confident in working in groups, thoughts may turn more towards the processes of interaction which abound in groups. In recognition of this we have included a section on group process (sometimes called group dynamics) which does draw on some elements of various theoretical systems.

The final meeting of a group needs to be handled with thought and care. In one sense, ending a group is a new and separate phase of group life, and so this aspect of running a group has been given its own small chapter, Chapter 7. Similarly, both during and after a group, evaluative appraisal is an important responsibility for the leader. Our final chapter sets out a very broad framework for the essential support of group leaders, and a basic approach to evaluation. We hope that readers who do go on to lead a group will feel encouraged to include evaluation in their 'duties', thereby ensuring a continuous process of further development.

1 Why support and why support groups?

The existence of this book should leave the reader in no doubt that the authors invest heavily in both the theory and research that identifies support as an important element in contemporary life. Further, we hold to the assumption that when good quality support is missing, there can be some very negative consequences in terms of physical health, mental health and general well-being. In combination with this we also invest heavily in the practice of using the group approach as an efficient means of providing support in many 'everyday' settings. It is appropriate, therefore, before beginning to discuss the practicalities of creating and running a support group, that both these assumptions be examined with a critical eye.

Why support?

In April 1996 an editorial in *The British Medical Journal* featured the interesting title 'Overwork can kill' (*BMJ* 1996). Of particular interest to us, however, is the sub-title which went on to state, 'Especially if combined with high demand, low control and poor social support'. Basically, this was a review and comment on a series of separate studies concerned with the health, illness and death of thousands of bus drivers, railway workers, and nurses across Europe. These studies combined unequivocally to identify high work load and job strain as a clear risk to health. Associated with this was the clear finding that has also become very familiar in health studies, namely, that, *'Mortality was significantly reduced in those who had good social networks and support, suggesting a buffering effect.'*

There can be little doubt from the many publications reporting this type of research that the term 'support' is acquiring a growing importance in current thinking concerning health and health risks. In fact, the term currently enjoys an expanded and frequent use in our general, daily lives. This was certainly not always the case though. Previously the word was probably heard mainly in architectural circles – a support being that element of a structure that had a special function in holding the rest of the building up. The term found a use in military, medical and political guises in later centuries and then was slowly incorporated into the disciplines of sociology and psychology in the twentieth century. From that point it made its way into journalism, literature and then popular usage. The overall humanitarian trend of our society since the 1930s has meant that our social administration is heavily geared to the provision of what is referred to as support in one form or another – sometimes financial, sometimes legal and sometimes as dedicated services aimed at improving human well-being. Common usage has now spread, for example, to football, cricket and athletics where players support each other and supporters give support to their teams. The ever present flow of events and situations in the world lead to demands for support that span from care-givers of the elderly through to victims of natural or man-made disasters. The world of professional health care, education and social care is now completely suffused with the notion of providing support to staff, trainees, students and patients. This trend ranges through most of the mainstream professions from teaching, nursing, occupational therapy, counselling and clinical psychology. Similarly, in industry, commerce and the civil service, personnel or human resource departments are increasingly to be found exploring options for the support of their workforce. To complete the survey we must note that so too, in everyday life, a friend may be regarded as 'supportive' or one particular member of a family can be referred to as the family support figure. Support is, we observe, an ever present concept in our modern lives.

One of the problems with a term that has such a wide application is that, although everybody basically knows what it means, the meaning actually becomes less exact and thus, quite often, a qualifying term has to be used in conjunction with the word. We now talk of logistical support for troops, financial support for people trapped in poverty, numerical support for new plays or favourite sports teams, and psychological or social support for those facing demanding or stressing circumstances. It is, of course, the latter meaning that is the focus of attention in this book.

Before launching into our main theme it is sensible to pause for a moment and consider the likely durability of this concept of support. It is a matter of observation that concepts can enjoy an era in which they are very fashionable and then slowly fade from use because they lose meaning along with the passage of time and progressive changes in culture. It would be unfortunate to find that the concept of support might be on such a track. One illustration, admittedly drawn from several centuries ago, serves our point well. Consider the concept of 'the soul and the afterlife'. In the Middle Ages, society was dominated by the clear certainty that our core sense of being persists after death in the form of an existence called a soul. Thus, what matters most in our physical life on Earth is to live in such a way as to guarantee that one's soul ends up in the right place after death. The literature, thinking, music and organization of society during the Middle Ages was heavily biased towards this idea – it was 'fashionable'. Today, though, religious affiliation has declined dramatically in many Western cultures and the actual concept of a soul is far less prevalent generally and greatly reduced in power as an influence on society. In this book we will be hoping to convince you of the importance of psychological support as a concept and of the value of providing support through the medium of group meetings. We make the basic assumption that support is important and effective in many human situations. Can we be sure, though, that this basic assumption concerning the positive effect and value of psychological support on our well-being is based on solid foundations and not a product of the vagaries of fashion and thus destined for the same fate as the concept of soul? Fortunately, it is not necessary to look very far to find substantial evidence and supportive (another use of the term) arguments. For example, two fields of research provide a great richness of material that suggests the notion of support as an effective influence in human life is solidly evidence based and, therefore, here to stay. First, the link between psychological support and physical health, and, second, the link between psychological support and mental health.

Psychological support and physical health

A brief clarification of terms may well be useful at this point. We use the term 'psychological support'. Many other authors and researchers use this too but, equally, the term 'social support' is also used. The terms are similar in meaning and, for our purposes in seeking to establish that support is likely to prove an enduring concept, have a high degree of overlap and are virtually interchangeable. Even so, brief comment on the way in which both terms are used is merited. Ganster and Victor (1988), writing under the title 'The impact of social support on mental and physical health', offer a straight-forward definition: 'Social support has been defined as the presence of others, or the resources provided by them, prior to, during and following a stressful event.' Ogden (2004) gives a detailed breakdown of the meaning of social support when it is used in a research context. She writes that what is generally referred to as social support assumes four elements: (1) interactions leading to an increase in self-esteem (through contact with others); (2) support through the provision of information; (3) social companionship; and (4) instrumental support (actual physical help). Clearly, this breakdown indicates a meaning close to that of psychological support. However, physical assistance is not necessarily a key aim of psychological support work and while formal information delivery may apply in certain types of support work and groups, it certainly will not apply in all cases. To clarify our own position on the meaning of psychological support, it is useful to specify an equivalent list of features that are likely to be on offer from a supportive individual relationship or an effective support group:

- the reduction of isolation through contact and interaction with others;
- the opportunity for confiding conversation that allows emotional expression and discussion;
- discourse that leads to an alteration in perception and outlook to a more balanced and positive mode;
- opportunities to enhance coping by learning from the experience of others.

It is fair to note that much of the epidemiological research mentioned below tends to talk of social support whereas authors dealing with practical and clinical applications of a helping or supportive type tend to refer to psychological support.

We began this section by citing the editorial in *The British Medical Journal* reviewing evidence of the link between support and health. Plenty of similar material now exists. Writing under the title *The Sickening Mind*, Martin (1997) produces a compelling review linking our life experience to basic health outcome as mediated by the functional efficiency of our immune system. The key point that Martin emphasizes is that the competence of the human immune system can increase or decrease in relation to a person's psychological status and well-being and, similarly, well-being can increase or decrease in relation to the level of psychological support that people enjoy in their life. As stated above, in this general context, psychological support is taken to mean a stable situation through which a person is able to experience confiding relationships that allow for emotional expression and in-depth contact. Such relationships offer the experience of being listened to and understood and impart the sense that the listener is available for help through information, discussion and empathy. It is not as simple as saying that if you are happy, then immunocompetence is up, and if you are without support, stressed and unhappy, it is down, but that is the general direction of findings. Scattered throughout Martin's thesis one finds a profusion of scientific studies, many of which give a clear indication that if a person is chronically deprived of the support normally provided through the medium of a stable confiding relationship, then measures of immune capability do show an associated decline, i.e. when psychological support is low, indices of immune functioning are lower too. He cites various research projects that assessed the negative impact on the immune system of the loss of support through the loss of close relationships. A good example here are a sequence of studies by Glaser and Kiecolt-Glaser showing that the death of a partner or the collapse of a marriage leading to separation and divorce are associated with lowered immune function – especially where the disruption of key relationships leads to loss of support. The details of these studies can be found in Kennedy et al. (1988).

Long-term research projects that follow through cohorts of people as-sessing and monitoring their general health, combined with recording the incidence and survival rates from illnesses such as heart failure and cancer, yield a similar pattern. Martin (1997) describes a large, now classic, long-term study based in California that assessed 5000 people over a period of years. This produced the clear finding that those whose life and lifestyle indicated the poorest levels of social contact and social support were twice as likely to die during the passing years than those with good supportive relationships. A Scandinavian study of over 17,000 people reached the same conclusion. One specific finding in the Californian study concerned women who had lives with poor quality relationships that offered little support. These women showed a significantly higher risk of developing most types of cancer than those with a good availability and quality of supportive relationships. Simi-larly, Williams et al. (1992), tracked approximately 1400 people with cor-onary artery disease (a condition that usually progresses into angina and eventually a heart attack) for a period averaging nine years. People who were rated lower on the provision and quality of social support, for example, un-married and without support in the form of good quality confiding re-lationships, showed a mortality risk that was three times higher than those with good support. The social support appeared to act as a 'buffer' against illness.

Ogden (2004) also writes on the theme of social support as a protective factor against ill health. In particular, she describes a large study of health and illness among East German refugees prior to the collapse of the East German regime and the removal of the Berlin Wall. Some 235 migrants were studied with health, employment status and social support being the key variables. The general conclusion of the study was summarized as, 'Therefore, ill-health was greatest in those subjects who were both unemployed and who reported low social support.'

This has been a fleeting glimpse taken from a great wealth of research and a huge literature that gives credence to the claim that psychological support is a meaningful concept and one that is likely to endure. It is now established beyond doubt that good levels of psychological/social support increase the probability of better physical health and better survival rates, should illness occur. Poor levels of psychological support, however, are associated with poorer health trends and lower rates of survival outcomes. Should readers need more detail, Baum et al. (1997) have produced an epic survey of health psychology research and practice that serves as a powerful resource on this theme.

Psychological support and mental health

The picture is very similar in the general field of mental health where the link between mental health and support has been well proven for several decades. There is, it has to be said, a dauntingly large literature in this field and we will mention just a tiny fraction. Early epidemiological studies established that poorer mental health is to be found in populations where levels of support are low. Miller and Ingham (1976) met and assessed over three hundred women in home interviews. They established that 'women reporting the lack of an intimate confidant had psychological symptoms of significantly greater severity than those reported by their more adequately supported counterparts'. Brown and Harris (1978), in a large and well-known research project, established that women who were victims of an acute, stressing life event, who did not have the benefit of a supportive, confiding relationship, were far more likely to suffer from depression than women who did have such support in their lives. The effect was very strong, indicating that depression at a level that merited treatment was more likely by a factor of four in women who lacked support. In their review of research some ten years after this study, Ganster and Victor (1988) list a series of similar studies showing a link between reduced psychological support, suicide, clinical depression and both acute and chronic anxiety.

Relationships that offer reliable and good quality support are, thus, frequently listed as a protective influence in research reports concerned with mental health. This theme is explored in depth by Halpen (2005) as part of a recent contribution from the field of community psychology. Writing under the general title 'Social Capital', he offers within this review a summary of what is now known concerning the impact that support, relationships, social integration, employment, etc. have on mental health and general well-being. Incidentally, employment is often included as a supportive influence since the work environment usually offers significant relationships and informal supportive networks of genuine substance. Surprisingly, although we might think that relatively modern research is the source of these basic findings on social and psychological support, Halpen points out that the early sociologist Émile Durkheim, writing in 1898, undertook a statistical analysis of social trends and was able to demonstrate quite clearly that suicide, for example, was much less common in people who had a good, stable relationship than in those who were separated or divorced. Even then, the 'buffering' effect of good relationships that included a component of support was a robust finding. In other words the effect is stable.

Of recent interest and of special relevance to the theme of this book, Halpen consolidates the position by noting that in 1999 'Harris et al. have shown, in a randomized trial on a sample similar to that covered in their original classic study, that volunteer befriending led to a significant reduction in depressive symptoms a year on compared with matched controls.'

More recently, the growth in the understanding of the post-traumatic stress reaction that many people experience following an unexpected traumatic incident, has led Joseph et al. (1997) to note that psychosocial factors can, to some extent, predict the persistence and severity of the reaction. Among these factors 'the recovery environment, e.g. social support' carries significant weight. The post-traumatic stress reaction can persist for years and cause serious and disabling mental health problems. Good support helps to reduce the risk of this happening.

Common events in physical health can have a negative impact on mental health. For example, Lane et al. (2002), in a study of nearly three hundred patients who had suffered a heart attack, found that 12 months after the event 37.2 per cent now suffered from depression and 40 per cent suffered from anxiety. However, Bennett and Connell (1988), in a useful study of 43 couples, one of whom had sustained a heart attack, clearly demonstrated that, 'The strongest predictors of partner depression were the emotional state of their spouse, the quality of the marital relationship and the *wider social support available to them*' (our italics).

We hope that the key point is now firmly established. The current frequency of use of the term support can be linked to enormous amounts of solid empirical evidence to show that support plays a significant protective role in the maintenance of physical and mental health and is also important as an aid to recovery from illness or trauma. Support matters in society generally as a 'buffer' against the psychological effects of social stressors. Our case, then, is that the concept of support is unlikely to turn out to be insubstantial and thus to fade with the vagaries of fashion. Equally, we can now say with complete confidence that, in view of all the above, awareness of the importance of support has to be increased and that the provision of support for the ill, injured, traumatized, mentally ill and stressed needs to be improved. Those who take the business of 'self-care' seriously should also be making sure that their personal arrangements for support are adequate.

The general call for support in relation to adverse experiences

In a companion publication to this book by one of the authors, a strong plea is made for improvements in the provision of psychological care for ill and injured people and their partners (Nichols 2003). As described, a significant component of psychological care is, of course, support. This plea by Nichols derived from many years of face-to-face clinical work as a health psychologist, in addition to the type of research described above. This combined experience led to the statement:

After meeting several thousand people who have suffered variously of a heart attack, renal failure, serious disability from back pain or arthritis, injury through surgical error or serious burns, been diagnosed as having cancer, lost a baby, developed difficult skin conditions and so on, it is just impossible to escape the fact that many of these people are frightened, disturbed or distressed by their experience and have a clear need for psychological care including improved support.

(Nichols 2004)

There are many other such calls for improved psychological/social support that come increasingly (and encouragingly it has to be said) in government publications. The latter are often in the form of 'National Service Frameworks'. These amount to an overview of the minimum standards of provision required within various medical specialties, for example, in the care of cancer and cardiac patients. As for the general literature, examples of findings that lead to a call for increased support are numerous. The situation of people recently discharged from intensive care following a period on life support after a traumatic accident or illness provides a good illustration. It has recently come to light that, when surviving on a ventilator under sedation, many people experience vivid and often alarming hallucinations. On discharge the memories of these hallucinations may persist for months, often being re-experienced as intrusive visual memories. It can be very disturbing when combined with all the other events that led to admission to intensive care. Skirrow et al. (2001) give a useful overview of the problem and make the call for improved assistance that includes post-discharge support for patients of this type. Similarly, Alexander (2004) argues that 'An explicit aim of palliative care is support for the family during the patient's illness and into bereavement.'

Sometimes people dealing with illness make a call for support themselves. Gillibrand (2004) conducted an inquiry with young diabetics that led to an expression of such a plea. She was investigating which psychosocial factors played a part in patients' ability to maintain good blood sugar control in insulin-dependent diabetes (without which microvascular deterioration can set in that leads to visual, renal and cardiac problems). Interestingly her two groups, one with poor blood sugar control and one with good control, were both clear on one issue, 'Participants in both groups indicated dissatisfaction with the diabetes clinics they attended and expressed a desire for change. This was expressed in terms of wanting a more age-specific clinic and *more emotional support.*'

Caring for a dementing person, whether that person is a partner or parent, may prove to be an exceptionally demanding experience. It can and often does lead to the progressive physical and emotional exhaustion of the care-giver. Certainly many care-givers willingly accept the role and often find fulfilment within it. In the long term, though, the inherent stressors that normally accompany the situation pose a real risk to both the physical and mental health of the care-giver. Briggs and Askham (1999) write on the needs of people who care for a partner with Alzheimer's disease. In general, the picture from people who have face-to-face involvement with care-givers is that of frequently encountered 'care-giver strain and stress'. The associated problems are not just simply concerning day-to-day home care but can include difficult transitions. For example, the processes of transferring the partner to a hospital or residential setting after years of home care. As one care-giver reported, 'Having taken sole responsibility for someone for many years, it is quite difficult to find suddenly that things have been taken out of your hands and that you are expected to take a back seat.' These authors argue for various interventions at all stages but resources can be very scarce and sometimes completely lacking. Inevitably, among the interventions called for, is the provision of a reliable support facility for care-givers involving both professional staff and experienced 'users' of such services in the past.

Linked to health care but in this instance concerning the vast numbers of *staff* that are involved, the issue of work stress and associated indications of the need for better support is a familiar theme for both the general press and professional literature. The plight of junior doctors or the burdens and stresses of heavily pressurized nurses has been a regular feature in both. This has been a long-standing problem. Writing under the title *Stress in Health Professionals*, Payne and Firth-Cozens (1987) edited a forward-looking book that anticipated many of the problems of the current era in health care. Their topics included stress in medical training, stress in the role of a general practitioner, stress in psychiatry (as we write, a mental health trust within the region has struggled through a period where a sizable proportion of its consultant psychiatrists have been off work with stress-related problems), stress among dentists and social workers and the stressing impact of new technology and the 'budget cutback' era. It would be absurd to argue that the entirety of the personnel involved, which is greater than a million, all need support and support systems. This is clearly not the case. However, it is well established that certain sectors of health-care work do impose very heavy burdens of responsibility together with significant emotional and physical drain. As Barraclough (1994) comments, concerning staff working with cancer patients, and Payne and Haines (2002) note in relation to staff in palliative care work, the demands of these roles can, at times, be exceptional and thus a good provision of individual and also group support is necessary to avoid problems of burn-out and emotional overload.

We have focused on health care as an area that provides plentiful examples of the need for support but, in fact, the call for improved support is common to a huge variety of different settings, not only health care. It is instructive to mention a few examples as a final element of the argument advocating the importance of support. In the field of education, teacher and student stress has become an issue that has led to calls for improved support. Cole and Walker (1989) identified what has been an increasing trend as the demands and classroom pressures within teaching have steadily increased. Currently there is a growing concern for the mental health of university students. Olohan (2004) reports a steady rise in emotional and mental problems among students while a useful article in *The Times* (23 April 2005) further illustrates the pressures for success and the financial plight of many students and urges more support. Hall and Lloyd (1993) give a graphic account of the pressures and stresses involved in dealing with women who had suffered sexual abuse as children. Counsellors, specialist social services workers, police and psychologists all fall under Hall and Lloyd's general statement,

> Working with survivors [of child sexual abuse] can be very rewarding for the helper, but, as we have seen, can bring strong and uncomfortable emotional reactions. ... There is a need for good support and supervision to be available for anyone who is working or planning to work with survivors.

Similarly, exposure to actual or vicarious trauma that can provoke a post-traumatic stress reaction is a situation in which good support can be of critical importance. Hence, police, firefighters, ambulance crew and volunteers involved in disaster work may encounter extremely disturbing experiences. In *The Psychologist* (April 2005) Sarah Davidson, a clinical psychologist, reported her early experiences as a Red Cross volunteer in Thailand after the Indian Ocean tsunami. She commented that British Embassy staff were working tirelessly with victims but were themselves at critical psychological risk. 'Although highly skilled, the embassy staff could not possibly have been prepared for the unprecedented nightmare unfolding before them ... We taught them basic psychological first aid and gave as much advice and support as we could.'

Finally, taking a wider look at workplace stress in general, Cartwright and Cooper (1997) talk of the 'growing epidemic of stress'. In their survey of workplace stress in Britain and other Western countries, a systematic analysis of the sources of stress proves very revealing. Work stress has always been with us, as research into the experience of employees in the Industrial Revolution quickly reveals. In those days it was the stress of appalling work conditions (in the mills and mines, for example), excessive hours and very low pay. Post-1980s, as Cartwright and Cooper describe, the nature of workplace stress has altered with the so-called enterprise culture. This situation can be found reflected in the now common phrase 'It is a high stress job.' The phrase evokes thoughts of work at an unrelenting pressure with the heavy burden of multiple tasks, responsibility for success through decisive management and marketing, meeting difficult targets, and so on. In reality, although this is true, the average worker who has very little control over their job and experiences constant low key pressure for little reward may be just as stressed. Also, as Cartwright and Cooper note, in the past decade or so many large organizations have undergone significant change that has driven both types of employees into high levels of disenchantment and stress. Which all takes us back to where we came in with the quotation from *The British Medical Journal*. It is now known that good support, individually delivered or through the device of support groups, can help protect people from the potentially damaging impact of workplace stress, organizational change and just sheer workload.

Our task thus far has been to give substance to our belief that support is an essential element in the maintenance of well-being, especially when people are facing times of high demand and stress. Our next task is to advance the argument that in certain cases the group format for providing support can be an efficient and, in some ways, superior resource.

Why groups?

The aim in this first chapter is to set the scene by presenting some basic ideas about support groups and the value that they offer. We hope to convince you that support groups make available a resource that is hard to come by elsewhere and that this resource has significance and relevance for people in many distressing or demanding circumstances. Our concern, therefore, is to show that support groups have a place in health care, education and the general care-giving context. There is also a place for support groups in certain work situations where staff are placed under heavy and demanding loads.

In order to develop our case, we will examine why people might be encouraged to join a support group, that is, what outcomes in terms of benefits and gains are believed to be available. Three different aspects will be considered: (1) our views on the benefits for the members of support groups; (2) our views on the benefits to the professions in having support groups as a resource for their clients; and (3) we will take a brief look at the experience and recommendations of other devotees of the group approach in providing support. Finally, to maintain a balanced outlook, we will inquire if there are any harmful or negative aspects of group work.

The group experience

When talking with colleagues who have not used group technique nor had personal experience as a member of a group, it is common to be asked the question, 'What is the point of groups and what do they offer that cannot be readily found by other means?' In fact, there are many different types of group and many different approaches to running them, each with its own special style, emphasis and objectives – so the answer can be quite lengthy. However, if pressed to justify why anyone should consider involvement with group techniques in simple, brief terms, then the explanation would centre on the notion of 'unique personal experience'. *The key point is that groups can provide certain direct personal experiences that can be extremely valuable in terms of personal development or personal support and, further, that such experiences are hard to come by other than through the group process. This applies equally to support groups or therapy groups.* Rather than expanding this with a breakdown of academic points an actual example of the group approach will serve rather better:

Case study The back pain support group

Our first case concerns a set of nine people who had suffered disabling back pain for some years and were eventually referred to the local hospital-based, Pain Management Service. Their ages, backgrounds and medical histories differed greatly. However, their paths converged to become one well known to all people who suffer chronic disabling back pain. Each had experienced a year or more of pain in the lower back usually with sciatic leg pain and tremendous soreness from stressed muscles that had gone into spasm around the pain site. The pain was such that bending, walking, sitting still for any length of time and general mobility such as twisting to gather something from the back seat of a car, had become activities that produced great discomfort and sometimes distress. Sleep was often badly disturbed by pain and 'getting going' in the morning could take half an hour or more because of great stiffness. Progressively they had all become rather slow-moving invalids, holding themselves stiffly and making only limited and very guarded movements – usually walking with a stick. None of the younger ones had kept their jobs, some being brought to a halt in the middle of a developing career or being compulsorily retired from military service. Significantly, most had become progressively socially isolated, withdrawing into a world centred upon pain and loss. Usually, after trying various combinations of pain-killers without much success, the family doctors involved, feeling equally frustrated, had lapsed into statements such as, 'Well, we can try the Pain Clinic but you may have to learn to live with it.' Not surprisingly, that particular communication often compounded a quietly growing fright captured in the thought, 'Is it always going to be like this?' As these people came to the Pain Management Service they were basically defeated – one or two managed a brave face but nevertheless they were struggling badly in the effort to keep going, often with a sense of despair and loneliness.

As is conventional these days, the Pain Management Service that they were referred to was multidisciplinary in nature with anaesthetists and physiotherapists providing the diagnostic and treatment element, a clinical psychologist to help patients to deal with the personal and psychological effects of their situation, and an occupational therapist to give further psychological support and practical help in rehabilitation. As is also often the case in such services, support group work was organized as part of the clinic facilities. Accordingly, after various visits on an individual basis to the clinic and various treatments including pain-killing drugs and physiotherapy, the nine patients were also invited to become members of a short-term support group that was to run for ten meetings.

In beginning this discussion on the rationale for the group approach, it will be instructive to explain why membership in this support group was considered to be both appropriate and advantageous for these nine people. What experiences were they expected to gain that they could not get elsewhere, and what was it that the staff who recommended their patients to attend the group sought by way of outcome?

It was hoped that a major benefit of the group would be in the support it offered, combined with the power it held to reverse some of the negative effects of withdrawal and isolation. Because of the general trend towards a narrower life and social withdrawal, these people had become trapped in their own negative views and beliefs about their situation. This meant that problem-solving in some had become limited and new initiatives were few. Often they admitted that they now had few objectives in life other than a day-to-day management of pain and the basics of living. This meant that there was little sense of direction or inclination to explore alternative approaches. Thinking was usually negative, focusing on the difficulties and obstacles of a life limited by chronic pain. Some, at least, had regular bouts of feeling injured and depressed because, it seemed, few people in their life genuinely understood their experience.

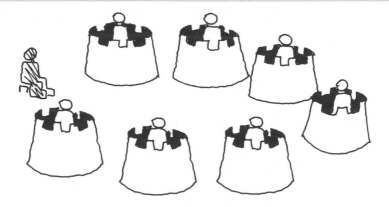

Figure 2 People become trapped in their own negative views

These hopes were, on the whole, realized for, within the group, most of the members found a new experience in being with eight other people who not only knew what life with chronic pain was like but experienced much the same themselves. They were all, therefore, able to give to each other something which no member of the care-giving team could truly give, that is, the shared solidarity of a distressing experience in common.

Of course, this is fairly obvious and in itself unremarkable. With a little luck, much the same would occur if, by chance, they had all happened to be together and had fallen to talking in the waiting room at the clinic. However, the important difference is that a working group of this type is guided by a set of objectives that specify the type of conversation that is valued and the type that is not. Thus, the nature of the relationships and the content of discussion in a support group can be very different from that which is usual in a waiting room. Waiting room conversations tend to be ritualistic and often centred on humour. They tend to edge away from anything that feels threatening or uncomfortable. In this group, the guidance was such that the members, in recounting their experiences, were encouraged to go beyond simple, everyday descriptive conversation and account for their behaviour and outlook by exploring the motive and perception behind it. Similarly, they were led to expand self-understanding by working at identifying personal feeling accurately, establishing what the feeling was truly directed towards and what perceptions the feeling was based on. According to the degree that each member was able to take on such tasks, he or she made a discovery, namely, that the act of self-disclosure in the presence of supportive others leads to a growth in self-awareness and understanding. This is referred to as *insight*. For example, one member who had been an army physical training instructor recounted how, if he saw an ex-colleague approaching him in the street he would step into a nearby shop to avoid him. Initially, he said that he did not know why he did this but, through discussion with group members about why he did this, he realized that indoctrination with army values had made him ashamed of physical disability. Although now discharged on health grounds, he still felt as if he was letting himself and the army down. The insight helped him think about why he had become depressed and possible new approaches to alleviate depression.

This all-important insight was generated partly through the process of self-disclosure itself and partly through the response and feedback of the other group members. It did not depend on brilliant insights by a leader. Further growth in self-awareness came for members when they took on a listening role too. In listening to the disclosures of the other people in the group, they either identified with the speaker or were able to make significant comparisons. Basically, they became more able to look at and understand their own reactions and behaviour in their situation. They also experienced the supportive presence and acceptance of the other members of the group. This proved a valuable 'platform' for some to think about and attempt changes in their lives and thus approach the problem of chronic pain in a different manner.

Some members later gave their views to the *Western Morning News*, a regional newspaper that ran a feature on the pain group:

(1) MP who had been a plumbing engineer, 'Before I came to the group I felt that life emotionally was just taking me deeper into a dark tunnel. But I found that I wasn't alone with my problems and that dreadful sense of isolation I had before was lifted. You find how to adopt a new mental approach and you begin to come out of that dark tunnel.'

(2) GP who had been an insurance agent, 'I got near to committing suicide – the group saved my life.'

Rather dramatic references perhaps, but nevertheless heartfelt and genuine and a useful illustration of the benefits possible in a support group.

Experiences in groups are often unique to groups. The group members, in contributing their experiences and giving honest, direct responses to one another, bring a richness of information and understanding that individual visits to the clinic may not match. In this context, each of these socially isolated, chronic pain victims was able to take part in constructing a resource that led to a unique personal experience for themselves and the other members. Individual psychological therapy could not compete in this specific respect, either in terms of resources or time efficiency – nine people benefited from the hour-long meetings, not just one.

Like people with other forms of disabling illness or injury, chronic pain victims often do live an increasingly narrow life centred around their pain. If positive change is to occur, the clients need to discover that they are responsible for a needless retreat. They need to discover that the price of retreat is more retreat, with a body musculature which becomes stiff and seized through lack of use and a social self that becomes less skilled and confident as a result of lack of normal social exchange. Life *can* be lived in a determined, outgoing way with positive experiences and forward direction, irrespective of the pain but it is hard to see this in isolation in your own home. It is a matter of changing perceptions and developing understanding. However, the beginning of change has to be the 'look into the psychological mirror' that the group process provides in order to discover what one has been doing, thinking and feeling – and why. This insight then facilitates change by bringing motivation for change and mutual encouragement as other group members struggle to develop similar new behaviour. The group thus acts as a protected space in which not only can the current self be seen with more clarity but the possibilities of new beginnings can be glimpsed.

While all this is going on, other aspects of group experience also feature

Figure 3 Life can be lived in a determined, outgoing way

in events. Support is one such aspect of most groups, whether they are designated support groups or not. This again is a product of group interaction, sometimes more so than dyadic (two-person) encounters. A group event is supportive if the recipient feels lifted and strengthened in some way. Thus, a woman describing a difficult week throughout which she had been very down and despairing went home from the group in lighter spirits, ready to give things another go. *No-one had given her special advice or therapy but the experience of being really listened to, allowed to express her feelings, sensing these feelings, being truly understood and valued by the others in the group and then given time to talk about the issue, challenged the despair and displaced it. She had been supported.*

Support is not unique to groups, of course, but in a good group it is ever present, in great abundance. Added to this, in more general terms, members of a group of the type just described tend to take on a mutual care role. This adds to the general supportive atmosphere and also makes an excellent platform from which a person can experiment with changes.

Closely allied to this is the sense of accountability which usually permeates a group of this type. Thus one member who had been absent for a meeting was asked, 'Why didn't you phone one of us if you were down? We've all agreed to make the effort – you're slipping back into your martyrdom thing again.'

Of course, the acid test for this theory is whether people actually do experience groups in the terms which we have described. This question, to be realistic, earns only a common-sense reply – some do, some do not. The situation is controlled by a complex interaction between the type of group and its objectives, the nature, style and skill of any particular leader together with the nature and responsiveness of any particular membership.

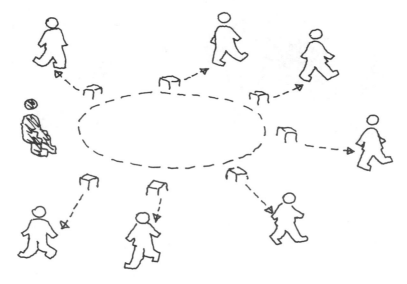

Figure 4 Home in lighter spirits

Generalizations across leaders, memberships and group types are of dubious value. Having declared this, our own working experience based on many, many differing groups (ranging from training and support groups with counsellors, doctors, dentists and nurses through to people in psychological distress or with disabilities resulting from pain or serious illness) gives both conviction and hope. Our first-hand finding is that if the group situation is carefully created for suitable members, things do indeed flow according to the theory. A significant proportion of the members gain in the expected way.

In a follow-up evaluation by questionnaire, one woman in the pain group wrote the following:

> It is hard to put into words what the support group was like. It certainly made me think a lot, in fact it filled my life for a while. I cannot remember specific events much but I'm different now. I still get depressed and cry at times, but not like I used to. That was disgusting, I feel ashamed of it. My attitude is different. I'm more outgoing and determined and have stopped brooding. The group gave me strength. I still need them all so I'm relieved that we have become an open self-help group now.

The general applications of support groups

Enough now of the pain group and the issue of its value, although the theme of value is picked up again in a later section. We have begun with a rather specific example. However, most of the points made above are in no way specific to support groups for chronic pain sufferers. They are a statement of some basic principles that will apply in modified form to groups operated for any people in stress, distress or dealing with demanding circumstances. Thus, further examples from the field of medicine alone would be of groups provided to support people distressed or disabled by arthritis, spinal cord injury, head injury and brain damage, insulin-dependent diabetes, amputation, severe burns, tinnitus, visual impairment, heart attack, multiple sclerosis and cancer, to name, literally, just a few possibilities.

Similarly, as implied in the previous sections, support groups have an equally important function with people exposed to the distress of others or carrying heavy burdens of care and responsibility. For example:

- parents of children with leukaemia;
- parents of children who die;
- pregnant women who suffer miscarriage;
- parents of brain-damaged children;
- partners of people who have suffered a severe stroke;
- partners of people who are victims of a heart attack;
- family care-givers for those with Alzheimer's disease;
- family care-givers for people with progressive neurological diseases (e.g., multiple sclerosis, motor neuron disease).

Llewelyn and Payne (1995) review the extent and impact of stress on care-givers and recommend the use of support groups to help deal with the problem.

As mentioned earlier, the *professional* roles associated with care-giving are often demanding emotionally or demanding in terms of workload. This issue was discussed generally by Bailey (1985). The demand for support work with nurses has grown by leaps and bounds since then. For example, Barraclough (1994) notes the stressing effects of working in oncology as a nurse and urges the provision of support systems. Similarly, Aranda (2004) writing under the title, 'The cost of caring', identifies many stressors that affect nurses working in palliative care. These include intense work pressure, constant exposure to death, lack of time to relax and grieve, exposure to the emotions of the dying patients and their close relatives and problems of burn-out and compassion fatigue. Again, attending a support group is high among the list of recommendations as part of a mix of coping strategies for the nurses involved. Clearly, the support group is regarded as a primary resource in providing for such needs.

Similar comments apply to the teaching profession as noted by Cole and Walker (1989) while doctors provide another obvious example (Firth-Cozens 1987). Professions not usually associated with caring but rather where members may experience unpredictable traumatic stress and need a period of support and personal assistance, have also begun to turn to the use of support groups. For example, civilian aircrew who experience a traumatic incident during take-off, flight or landing are encouraged to use discussion and support groups during the months following the incident (Johnston 1985). Similar trends are to be detected with the police and fire service. The general issue of support and support groups following traumatic stress is discussed very well in Raphael (1986).

There has been no attempt here to be exhaustive in compiling a list of the possible applications of support groups. Obviously each field will generate its own list. However, we make the point that we are not alone in recommending serious consideration for the use of support groups in a very wide variety of settings.

Key concepts

Support groups of the type we will be describing take the generic term *helping groups*. Lakin (1985) has written a comprehensive text of the same name. He traces the development and history of helping groups and specifies the full range of group types that fall under this term, including self-help groups which have no trained or formal group leaders. Essentially, the power of helping groups is centred on the act of bringing people together to create the group environment and thus group processes. Lakin observes, 'We see that the helping group offers multiple sources of support and that support comes primarily from peers rather than the credentialed expert.' This should not be taken to infer that the group leader is virtually redundant, by the way, since a set of people simply put together with no sense of how to behave in order to bring about effective group processes may well not achieve much by way of consistency and quality of support. Such a group can easily slide into confusion, or adopt unhelpful patterns. The members bring the basic resource, that is their presence, contributions and reactions but the leader's function is equally important. Guiding, modelling, shaping and preserving safety with forward direction, he or she provides the catalyst which can make the difference between sterility and productive benefit. Lakin's view of the core mechanisms of the helping group runs close to our own given in the example of the pain group:

> The general mechanisms of group helping are group acceptance in return for self-disclosure, mutual comparison, mutual support and interpersonal feedback. The leaders may model candid and constructive reactions to members. Group support and interpersonal feedback provide benign pressure for personal change.

You will note here an indication of the self-powering nature of groups. People bring a powerful need to be accepted into their group, particularly when in distress and meeting fellow victims who are capable of understanding and caring. When the members have an understanding of the objectives and valued behaviour within a group, then, to a degree, a self-guided system is created. Individuals are accepted when they meet group objectives such as honest self-disclosure and self-exploration.

Definitions and features

There seems little point in struggling to advance watertight definitions of the helping group. There are many possible variants. Our concern, now clearly established, is primarily with the type of helping group known as a support group which will comprise a membership of somewhere between four and twelve people together with a facilitator or leader. These people will usually share some common identified need and will have recognized the existence of that need so that they will be prepared to attend a relevant group as a possible means of dealing with it. In addition, these people will be capable of giving reciprocal care to other members of the group. *The support group is about mutual help.*

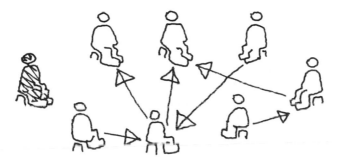

Figure 5 The support group is about mutual help

As for composition, the examples cited so far have all been of homogeneous group membership; all post-traumatic stress, all nurses, all counsellors, etc. This is by no means a vital feature, though. Support groups may readily be formed on a heterogeneous basis as long as there is sufficient common ground between members to allow the uptake of a collective task and sufficient experience in common to allow meaningful sharing, empathy and support. Therefore, a number of people receiving psychiatric care related to differing problems such as anxiety reactions, depressive disturbances and addictive states, would usually make a suitable mixed group membership. It would be a clear mistake, though, for a social worker seeking support related to her work to join such a group – the needs would be too discrepant. The issue of group membership is dealt with in Chapter 5.

The content of support groups

In the same way that we have avoided specific definitions of the helping group, it is also worth avoiding attempts to give an exact prescription for the activities within support groups. Clearly it is insufficient to describe the activity simply as people helping one another – this could apply equally well to people at a bus stop. The basic notion, as we have shown in the example of the pain group, is of a range of activities, or rather, exchanges between people, that promote self-awareness, change and support. Now these exchanges can and will be pursued at varying levels of intensity. Various factors govern this level of intensity, including the degree of safety which the members feel, the skill and maturity of the group leader in communicating and modelling group objectives, the lifespan of the group which determines the time available for learning by the members and, consequently, the extent to which the members make a committed, non-defensive investment in the development of the interactions and skills of group life. In practicable terms, these all-important skills may be described as:

- learning to focus on exchanges related to issues of personal relevance rather than social rituals and 'pastimes';
- learning to confront 'difficult' issues rather than denying these or retreating behind superficiality;
- developing the skill of reflective, feeling-based self-disclosure;
- learning to use the responses, feedback and challenges of other group members to develop self-awareness;
- assisting other members with these tasks;
- learning to receive and give support.

We will refer to this cluster of skills as the 'core interactions'.

As you can see, the group is a micro-culture with its own ways and values. These objectives would be desperately out of place in certain other settings but they are basically what groups are about. Each person will differ in his or her ability to absorb and pursue the objectives. There may be a form of culture shock and some will find that initially it makes them feel very vulnerable and threatened, and so will retreat into near silence, or use a façade such as ceaseless jocularity as a defence. Hence, returning to the concept of intensity, if a group, or a significant proportion of its members, does not understand these objectives or fails to be at peace with them, then the intensity and frequency of on target interactions (i.e. those listed above) will be low. Similarly, a leader who has not achieved such development will probably produce much the same situation. Hence the logic of our Chapters 3 and 4.

Individual groups may be graded on a scale representing the intensity and frequency of these core interactions. For example, a support group composed of the partners of stroke victims was run by a community nurse who had little training or experience in group work. It had a scheduled life of only six meetings. This we will compare with a support group for professional counsellors which had run for some years. It had monthly meetings and was led by a person with considerable training and over ten years of experience in leading groups. The counsellors group scored high on the scale of intensity and frequency of core interactions – very little of its time was spent on anything else. It was a 'well matured' group. In contrast, the combination of an insecure leader, short group life and people new to groups meant that the stroke partners group spent much more time off target and tended to remain defensive and superficial. Nevertheless, they did engage to a degree in the core interactions and were clearly an effective support group. This last point needs to be emphasized. While the group run by the nurse scored lower on intensity, it did not mean it was of limited value. Such is the power of the group experience that most of the members gained great benefit in terms of basic support, the opportunity for sharing and the ventilation of feelings together with companionship in stress. Worthwhile indeed.

One final point concerning the broad context of groups. The activity within a helping group must be tailored to the range of needs of the clients. Sometimes, as with the pain group, the need is for accurate knowledge or information as well as support. Thus, some part of certain sessions was devoted to wholly different work such as teaching and information transmission. The effective leader will ensure that needs are assessed and priorities ordered accordingly. Sometimes other activities must take precedence over group discussion as a matter of straightforward, practical necessity.

Other types of group work

This volume is primarily intended as a practical guide and encouragement to those in professional, care-giving roles who seek to extend their care by setting up a support group. The emphasis is practical and, thus, priority of space goes to the practical aspects which are likely to matter in the first-hand experience of running a support group. This section is intended to provide background information. However, because it leans towards the academic in being concerned with classification, it will be basic and brief.

There are, of course, various classificatory systems of group types which are usually linked to an appraisal of group aims and function. Although such classifications might be seen to be of minimal relevance to those of you who are thinking of running a basic support group, it can sometimes be helpful to have a clear awareness of the various uses to which group technique is put. One justification for this view is that it is helpful at times to keep limits in mind; another is that it will reduce confusion to know that you run a particular type of group and have no obligation to imitate some other type. Brown (1986) lists eight general types of group. Based on his breakdown we can list the five most relevant:

- *Assessment groups*: where the concern is to gain information concerning the members' abilities, behaviour and needs.
- *Support and maintenance groups – the helping group*: The subject of this book.
- *Change or therapy groups*: here the emphasis is on personal education or therapy of some sort. In personal education it can be the case that the people involved are not seeking psychological help as such but need a resource for further personal learning and development, because of career demands perhaps, e.g., trainee counsellors, doctors or members of other caring professions. Often, though, therapy groups in this category are directed to providing therapy for people with particular psychological problems. The range includes social skills and assertiveness training groups, anxiety and stress management groups, personal growth groups, etc.
- *Education, information and training groups*: e.g., pre-natal groups.
- *Collective change groups*: here the unit of alteration is not the individual but a collection of related people, most obviously the family. A typical example is that of family therapy groups.

Many readers will have encountered various names given to group practice, for example, gestalt groups, psychodrama groups, rational emotive therapy groups, transactional analysis groups, and so on. These are, in fact, names denoting theoretical and stylistic emphases in group work but nevertheless they still fit into the scheme above. Psychodrama, for example, is a technique which may be used in either helping or personal education groups. The technique is a way of optimizing the exploration of feeling and uses the technique of dramatic re-enactment to facilitate emotional analysis. The objective of these types of groups is familiar to us already, namely self-disclosure and insight.

It can be confusing for someone new to group work when confronted by the competing claims of these techniques and apparently required to make a commitment to an approach. Our view is that the best beginning is an open-ended stance without commitment to a style – eclecticism in other words. People are quite capable of meeting together in a support group without it having a special emphasis. It is also useful to remember that most of these high-profile techniques were spawned in the commercial atmosphere of

American clinics. They have much of value to offer but the differences between them are often more apparent than real and are sharpened for purposes of commercial competition.

More on the value of groups

The opening section of this chapter sought, in a general way, to demonstrate certain aspects of the special value of groups. The discussion was not complete and since this is another area of knowledge with which an intending group leader should have a clear familiarity we will further extend the points made (since unless the benefits are clear it would hardly be professional to launch into group work). There are two perspectives to consider: (1) the client's perspective; and (2) the group leader's perspective.

The client's perspective

Yalom, an American group psychotherapist, is known for his list of so-called 'curative factors' in group therapy (Yalom 1985). These are now considered to be generally available benefits of the group environment and group experience that are likely to affect the individual member in a positive way. Yalom was writing, it has to be said, with reference to therapy groups rather than support groups *per se*, but again there is such overlap that much of his list applies. The following extracts identify and illustrate parts of his list which clearly apply to our concerns – they have great relevance to the pain group, for example. People in support groups benefit from the following factors.

- *Group cohesion* – a powerful sense of belonging and acceptance.
- *Universality* – discovering that one's feelings and experiences are to be found in similar form among others in the group, i.e. one is not as alone as it seemed.
- *The instillation of hope.*
- *The corrective recapitulation of the family group* – that is, belonging again in the 'family' of a group where reality testing and honest feedback are possible, e.g., How do I appear to others? Do I really think in the same way as him? Have I given up as much as they say? Are they really like my beliefs suggest?
- *Imitative behaviour* – people can learn vicariously, simply listening and watching while another member goes through his or her difficulties which are then discussed. This can play a significant part in the development of insight and initiation of change.
- *Intellectualization* – growth in knowledge and understanding of one's own psychology.
- *Catharsis* – the opportunity to express and share feeling with others, to bring one's tears and anger to the group and have them received.

> Such expression of emotion can produce an enormously freeing and uplifting effect, releasing energy which had been used to suppress the (previously) unacceptable feelings.

Essentially, these curative factors reflect the basic ingredients of support and the growth of self-knowledge which we presented earlier as the rationale for the group approach. There is no guaranteed provision, of course. Depending on the group atmosphere and its general pattern, together with each member's level of involvement, things may go well or go badly, in which case the positive benefits will be reduced.

The true strength of the support group experience is best illustrated with reference to the cohesion and the intense social engagement that groups can bring about. Many of the people who actually need to join a helping group will have been in a state of some retreat from the social world. This can apply to people, say, with problems of social anxiety or depression or those dealing with a major loss such as spinal cord injury and paralysis. Equally, people who have become home-based care-givers can drift into relative isolation too, as the pressures of their seven days a week care role intrudes. Support groups offer, through the social cohesion that develops in groups, a means of challenging such social isolation. To extend this point we will consider the effects of the home-based care-giving role in a little more detail.

A proportion of people who take on this role, whether with handicapped, elderly or seriously ill people, run the risks of a problem labelled by Nichols (2003) as the 'Care Trap'. Early on, a trend that rapidly restricts life can set in. This trend centres around the carers' efforts to be maximally protective and caring. In the case of major illness, this is often driven by a degree of guilt in relation to the carer's own unimpaired health and mobility combining with a deep compassion. As a result, a pattern of over-committed care can develop, with a serious loss of independence and freedom for personal interests. General freedom for time outside of the home also becomes a thing of the past. In a specific example encountered recently, an outgoing middle-aged woman took on the care of her husband who was suffering minor strokes as a result of cerebral vascular deterioration. He was almost unable to walk. She tried to deal with her protective needs by almost always being on hand, within calling distance, that is. If she left the house it was in a very brief, anxious, rushed manner, 'in case he has an attack while I'm gone'. As the months went by, her social activity and friendships lapsed. She had abandoned her own needs for social contact and interesting activities and thus became virtually housebound and isolated by her pattern of excessive, anxious care. In a sense the 'living had gone out of her life' – a classic case of the Care Trap.

Isolation of this type has an insidious, destructive effect, almost like a veil slowly cutting off the rest of the community. It can be a lonely, dull and sad existence. Fortunately the lady was persuaded by a community nurse to join a support group for the partners of stroke victims. The support group was a totally contrasting experience for her that gave great uplift. Once more she had intense involvement with people. There was a regular afternoon a week with conversation, interest, companionship, laughter – a friendship network through the telephone, a time to look forward to in each week and the feeling of being bonded. Somehow the formal analyses of group benefits do not capture this element. To put it in everyday language, it is something to do with bouncing back into life – into the world of people, chatter and *belonging*.

The group leader's perspective
One assumption that we make is that many of the people who will use this book are in a professional, care-giving role already. Part of the motivation for bothering with the book may well be a sense of 'I ought to do more' or 'we are offering so little and are stretched to the limit at that'. Often there is a need to provide more effective support but little opportunity so to do.

Case study The cardiac rehabilitation nurse
A cardiac rehabilitation nurse was responsible for the care of people who had been discharged home from a hospital after surviving a heart attack. The nurse was required to function as their support figure and coordinate their rehabilitation programme. Although not referred to her in the strict sense of the word, she also felt a responsibility for their partners. She worried in particular about the partners because they were often under great strain and needed separate attention that she was rarely able to give because of time constraints. Despite misgivings about lack of training, she organized a support group. It was the right move. Instead of stretching herself even more thinly in an effort to increase brief, individual contacts, the group setting allowed her to spend a good hour a month with the partners. She could hear their difficulties, join in giving support, offer advice and take note of needs that had to be dealt with in a practical way. It gave the nurse a sense of having created something productive. Most of all, she felt the burden of demand being lifted and was greatly reassured to watch the cohesiveness of the group growing, with the group's sources of encouragement and support bolstering her own efforts.

Similarly, if we may continue to make points by way of examples, consider the case of a college counsellor who, among his client list, received at least half a dozen students who were socially withdrawn and complained of loneliness since they could not seem to make friends. Individual counselling sessions did, of course, have a significant part to play but the sessions lacked the element of direct experience. The counsellor could not actually observe their pattern of social interaction and had only the beliefs of the students to work on. Nor could the students gain much by way of direct feedback and encouragement in individual counselling sessions that might have assisted them in the problem. With such social difficulties it is the perception of others and beliefs about oneself that tend to be at the root of the problem of withdrawal. An interactive group such as a support group whose objective is to learn by the experience of doing offers just the direct personal experience that individual counselling sessions lack. Please do not take this as an attack on individual counselling – the remarks are specific to this example and even here individual counselling would be a great asset as a pre-group preparatory event. It was for this reason that the counsellor ran a regular support group for students. It extended the range of help which he could offer tremendously, by making available alternative and direct means for personal change and development.

As a last brief example, it will be helpful to reflect for a moment on the task that befalls one of the authors, namely to assist general practitioners towards a better understanding of the interpersonal aspects of the doctor–patient relationship. The tendency with medical education is always to make 'them' or 'the patient' the focus of attention, never 'me, the doctor'. Probably the least developed aspect of medical training is that aspect which covers the doctor's own psychology and, therefore, interpersonal relations and behaviour with patients. This is regrettable since training and working as a doctor are complex psychological events which, in the view of both authors, often lead to psychological changes which are very disadvantageous to doctor–patient relationships and doctor–staff relationships. Again, the problem arises that simply lecturing doctors produces only a weak probability of positive change. An effective group experience has much greater potential, though. Within a support and learning group, a receptive doctor will encounter a little of his or her own psychology actually at work – a powerful and instructive learning experience since, in everyday life, we rarely have conscious access to certain aspects of our own functioning. Thus, a person who has to teach doctors on the theme of interpersonal relationships has a greatly strengthened hand if he or she can successfully engage the doctors' commitment to work at a group experience to a level of intensity where the 'psychological mirror' begins to reflect back at them and self-discovery begins. It is most unfortunate that doctors in their early training are sometimes taught to eschew any emotional reactions in themselves, these being branded as professional weakness. In fact, the emotions that they find themselves experiencing in their consultations or patient care may be a first-hand and intense indication as to what is most troubling the patients. Even a simple but well-run support group can prove an effective learning experience that challenges emotional repression in young doctors.

In these three examples a common theme emerges. The support roup approach a valuable resource in care-giving, therapy, and personal education.

It offers certain unique experiences which extend the professional care-giver's/ educator's capacity to be of help or bring about the change. It thus directly assists people in the type of professional roles that we used as examples. Rounding off this commentary on the benefits of support groups, we will return to Brown (1986). He, too, set his mind to the task of enumerating the special benefits of group technique. There is good agreement with our own position emphasizing support and the potential for attitude, feeling and behaviour change through direct experience and the 'shaping' power of the group process. However, he also includes the following:

- Groups are time-efficient for the professional worker.
- Certain clients are more comfortable in a group setting, finding the unrelenting intensity and intimacy of individual counselling/ therapy uncomfortable.
- The ratio of members to therapists alters the power position to a more democratic basis. The client thus has more opportunity to exert influence than in individual work.
- Every member is a potential helper.

On the use of support groups

The sheer weight of 'clinical' evidence and consumer feedback that validates the usefulness of support groups is enormous and more than enough to remove doubts about the essential issue, namely that support groups are an effective, credible, and worthwhile resource in giving care and support in a hugely diverse number of situations. We may be a little slow in fully utilizing this potential in Britain however. There are support groups to be found, of course, but we cannot claim that they are routinely on offer in hospitals, mental health trusts, education or industry. In fact, as far as general impressions go, rather than being widespread, the use of support groups is fairly patchy in this country. As a comparison, Hossack and Wall (2005) mention survey reports of 'between 7.5 and 15 million people attending US support groups addressing almost every known mental health issue'. A rather different scenario.

It should be pointed out that we are not alone in our call for the greater use of support groups. There are many studies in which both patients, clients and people in professional or research roles make a similar call based on working experience or research outcome. For example, Finlay (1993), writing under the title *Groupwork in Occupational Therapy*, advocates wider use of groups by occupational therapist in their various settings. Hall and Lloyd (1993), in their extensive review of approaches to helping women survivors of sexual abuse, suggest support group work either as an alternative to individual therapy work or as part of a sequence of stages in working through the trauma. It is of note that, even in this very specialized setting, the advantages of the support group for women are substantial. Drawing on their own experience Hall and Lloyd list the main advantages as given below. This list tends to validate the general positive features of groups specified earlier:

- Women can share the burden of abuse with others of similar experience.
- Emotional and social isolation is reduced – 'I am not the only one.'
- The group helps women face the reality of what has happened.
- The group reveals feelings of guilt, anger, grief and loneliness to be normal.
- Established members can encourage others by relating their progress.
- It is a place of safety to express true feelings.
- The women can work together to build trust and alleviate guilt.

Similarly Payne et al. (2004) urge palliative care nurses to consider support groups as part of a strategy of self-care with a view to dealing with the stresses of the job while Rawle et al. (2005), having researched the reactions of patients in differing cardiac rehabilitation regimes, found a preference for a conversation-based, patient-led support group format. Patients in a recently conducted pain management programme indicated a positive evaluation of the support group element, Quigney and Callaghan (2005). Briggs and Askham (1999) similarly promote the importance of support groups for the care of people with Alzheimer's disease.

As a final example, an interesting piece from Canada deals with support groups for cancer patients and makes a very strong case. Yaskowich and Stam (2003) summarize their findings by noting:

> Interviews with participants and leaders of support groups were used to theorize the importance of support to cancer patients with varying stages and length of disease. Patient interview led us to describe the process of joining, belonging and identifying with support groups as an important process ... encompassing a search for a 'separate social space'.

These authors discover through interviews that the cancer patients that they worked with gained from their groups because the group promoted hope and a demystifying of their situation by offering an alternative social contact with an inherent safety that allowed different types of conversation. As one participant patient stated:

> When you really stop to think of it all, it's very overwhelming – and I guess that's why the support group is so good, because everybody's in

the same boat, so we're able to talk about the overwhelming feelings and fears and death – you just can't tell everybody those things.

This powerful personal statement captures much of our argument. Put together with reasonable forethought and planning, operated in a sensitive helpful way that provides an assured atmosphere of safety and support, most people can gain from membership in a support group. Those in some kind of difficult circumstance in life will usually gain a very great deal.

Is it all roses or can groups do harm?

Speaking of groups in general, including therapy groups, we have to be balanced and ask this question. What is the possibility of experiences in groups having a negative impact on certain types of people, or people in certain types of situation? The short answer has to be, no, it is not all roses forming and running a group – they can go wrong and they can do harm. That is why this book will urge over and over again the adoption of a cautious, reflective approach.

Perhaps in the initial effort to encourage interest in the support group approach, this chapter has erred a little towards the 'hard sell'. Now is the moment, therefore, to lodge one or two qualifications, so take this section as the 'small print'.

Groups do not always go well

Despite the best of intentions, groups of people are not always as compliant in behaving and responding as one hopes they would be. It does not happen frequently but we have both known sessions of otherwise successful groups which have become silent and tense, or angry and disturbed. Such occasions are not necessarily unproductive but they can be uncomfortable and hard work for the group leader, particularly if it is a new experience. Similarly, we have both known groups which have basically failed from start to finish. This again is not a common event but be assured it does happen. If, for one reason or another, the group begins to feel threatened and stays that way, then it will probably persist as a defensive, evasive group, retreating into silence, or using the device of trivialization as an escape. Needless to say, this can prove a fraught experience for the leader – it is difficult not to become despondent and frustrated in such circumstances, hence it is useful to have a supportive discussant who takes part in occasional review sessions with the leader.

We feel it necessary to be philosophical about these risks rather than alarmed by them. Personal experience suggests that difficulties of this type are much less likely with the straightforward support group composed of people in some distress. A more likely risk area is with support or interpersonal training groups composed of group-naïve but otherwise sophisticated professional people. They may find the personal exposure and direct feedback of the group somewhat threatening and respond accordingly. Again, drawing on personal experience, groups composed of health-care professionals, for example, are more likely to get themselves into difficulties if there are senior colleagues mixed with junior colleagues. Later on in the volume we will be thinking about the composition of groups and we will expand on these comments. For now, do not take this as a 'no go' warning. Groups with professional people can be extremely rewarding and successful. We are simply saying they do not inevitably go well – it is not always roses.

Despite careful selection some members may prove to be unsuited

As opposed to difficulties with the group as a whole, a further hazard is that of starting off a group and discovering that one or more of the members cannot cope and either becomes disturbed by the group or, conversely, begins to disrupt and disable the group. This can be dealt with in various ways, assuming that group pressure or support itself is insufficient. Chapter 6 takes up this theme.

Outside influences may interfere

One thing to remember about groups is that both the members and the leader can bring feelings and thoughts into a meeting that do not belong to the transactions of the meeting, as a result of either conscious or unconscious motives. This can change the character of the meeting. Sometimes this is referred to as 'emotional luggage'. For example, a woman arrived at her group after a heated exchange with her male manager at work. Although she told everybody about the event and it was apparently ventilated and forgotten, many of her interventions that evening were of an angry type. In particular, she became very cross with the leader (who was also male).

On another occasion, a group leader arrived at a meeting in what can best be described as a tired and dismal mood. He had no real wish to conduct a group at all that day. In fact, under the terms by which the group was run (he was a participant-leader, i.e. he joined in the general exchanges within the group as well as offering leadership), he should have shared his feelings immediately, worked through them and used the group presence to advantage. He unwisely chose not to, feeling that he wanted to keep his feelings contained. As a result, his involvement was listless, which the group sensed. It led to the meeting being fairly ineffectual and, furthermore, one of the members who had given small signs that she was in some distress with personal problems, was completely overlooked. She went away feeling hurt and neglected.

Leaders make mistakes

In this example, you meet the last thorn on the rose bush which we will mention. It is a simple fact of groups – 'leaders sometimes mess things up'. Excessive intervention, inadequate guidance, attempting to push the group a way it does not wish to go, failing to read the signs, and so on. Experienced group leaders learn to live with this as a fact of life. They will maintain sincerity, integrity, and concentrate as best they can, but once in a while they accept there will be an error. For example, a group of trainee social workers was unusually inhibited and evasive. The leader attempted to introduce an exercise to promote increased depth of self-exploration. It was an error of judgement. The exercise exceeded the threshold for the group. What little safety they felt was destroyed. One of the members (who later revealed that he was homosexual) stormed out in a rage. The next hour was difficult but the atmosphere eventually settled, the cross member returned with an apology, perceptions and experiences of the incident were exchanged and finally the group settled down productive work. The leader got away with it but it had been a definite mistake.

Figure 6 Exceeding the threshold for the group

In specific circumstances there is a risk of harm

Now to the issue of actual harm. As far as personal appraisal goes, neither of us has any first-hand experience or knowledge to suggest that individuals have come to harm in carefully run helping groups in which the leaders have the maintenance of a caring atmosphere as a major priority – quite the opposite, in fact. The same applies to support group work with professional staff. However, there is a literature with evidence to show that certain kinds of *personal learning* group, encounter, gestalt, etc., can adversely affect a small proportion of people. As Lakin (1985) describes, it has been established that a small proportion of people attending encounter-style personal growth groups are basically left worse off for their trouble in the sense that they find the experience unpleasant or are made emotionally more agitated by the event. Also, some observations suggest that a type of training group fashionable in the UK, known as a group analytic training group, can be extremely disturbing to people who have no preparation at all for the experience and whose suitability has not been ascertained (Nichols 1976).

The general understanding of schizophrenia these days places some emphasis on helping people who are in remission from a schizophrenic episode to follow an emotionally quiet lifestyle. Research and clinical observation shows that emotionally stirring atmospheres increase the likelihood of a further breakdown occurring. Obviously, then, support group work for people with a background of serious mental illness is to be avoided other than by specialists in the field.

Lakin (1985) also has an interesting section in his text under the heading 'Group power – for good and for ill'. In this the potential for harm and destabilization is well illustrated. For example, where a person's need for acceptance by a group is actually met with rejection, where the pressure for change and corrective feedback propels an individual into ways of behaviour for which he or she has inadequate resources, or where the pressure for self-disclosure clashes with a fear of exposure and evaluation. These can be damaging experiences. It is a section worth reading. However, we will qualify the position by stating that an observant, caring leader will work to adjust the group process in order to protect people in real difficulties. It is also the case that this kind of eventuality relates more to personal learning and therapy groups than basic support groups. Our view is that in the type of groups we will deal with in the rest of the book, *good leadership means protective, caring leadership* – not over-protective but adequately protective. Proper selection, suitable pace and adequate protection will ensure that the possibility of harm to any individual in the group will be minimized.

Finally, it was mentioned much earlier that a group is a micro-culture. Most people already belong to one micro-culture, their family. A problem arises when one member of a family has experiences which lead to significant change (as in an interpersonal relations training group) while the other members do not. In adopting the values and norms of a group it can happen that a person becomes alienated to a degree from their family, because the family cannot function like group members. The same can happen in the workplace. It is worth bearing in mind and raising as an issue on a preventive basis in ongoing groups. The good group leader will thus also have a caring awareness for people whom he or she will never meet in the group.

Do group leaders need training?

Ideally, no-one should run a group without having had first-hand experience of participation in a group, without having acquired a relaxed familiarity with the group atmosphere and without having found his or her confidence with the usual activities in groups (in particular, presenting personal issues and exploring the feelings associated with these). This would be the barest minimum. Being even more idealistic, an intending leader would have spent time in a specially designed training group backed up by theory classes and followed by a period of apprenticeship-style supervision in running the first groups. Where, however, does this leave, say, our hospice nurses who want to set up a support group for themselves next month, or the audiologists who

Figure 7 Support helps

wish to start a regular group meeting for tinnitus sufferers, or the occupational therapists who see the need for a helping group to assist amputees and paraplegic people? In reality, there are no readily available training programmes to give them all the ideal start. Should these people steer clear of groups then? The very clear message behind this volume, indeed the basic reason for writing it, is that we believe such a conclusion is unnecessary. We hope to establish an approach, and, more importantly, an attitude to the approach which will allow professional people cautiously to edge into group work. We will emphasize caution, certain elements of personal preparation, the use of a discussant/supervisor and an effort to gain personal group experience. However, we will try to communicate sufficient knowledge and 'know-how' such that, combined with a professional attitude, it should be possible to run a valuable, if basic, helping group. Once engaged in running a group, it provides a powerful teaching experience itself as long as one remains receptive and discusses events with a colleague who has some experience too.

2 Support groups in action

This chapter gives a wider review of various circumstances in which support groups are used. Our objective in putting this together is to help you to judge whether the needs in your particular situation are in some way similar to those revealed in the examples to follow. If so, you then have to decide whether or not you wish to advance to the stage covered in Chapter 5, that is, setting up a group and conducting the first meeting.

The illustrations are, you will note, quite wide-ranging. A couple of them will be familiar from Chapter 1 and are extended in this chapter. Some of the groups described offered simple support work with distressed clients. Others, like the counsellors' group and the group for GPs, involved support work combined with an element of personal learning (that is, expanded knowledge concerning one's needs, fears and defences).

Example 1 A post-coronary support group

The immediate care following a heart attack is normally given by specialist coronary care units. Here attention is primarily directed to physical care and priority is given to returning the damaged heart to normal function. Later, clients may be transferred to general wards for continuing recovery. On average, discharge home will take place around about two weeks after the heart attack. It can be a very disturbed time both for the person who has been ill, perhaps having literally faced death. It is also a difficult and stressing time for the partner and close family.

Generally speaking, most of us hold an unrecognized assumption that good health will continue in life. A heart attack brings about a traumatic collapse of such confidence. People realize that there is a high risk of further attacks and often believe that a return to normal life carries hidden threats. It can feel safe enough being nursed in a coronary care unit but the discharge home can lead to tremendous insecurity since it means that immediate help is no longer at hand. This is why it is such a major stress experience, some-times leaving entire families feeling vulnerable and apprehensive.

This is not of course new knowledge. For some years now post-coronary rehabilitation programmes have been discussed as a means of helping people deal with these circumstances more effectively. They are also seen as a way of extending support beyond the immediate period of hospitalization. Typically such rehabilitation efforts combine an exercise and education programme with a group support element. In these terms, they are a good example of basic support groups.

Post-coronary support groups either function in a 'rolling' style, with members continuously joining and leaving or, alternatively, use a 'batch' approach. The latter involves a fixed membership with each programme and group lasting six to ten weeks. The example chosen involves the 'rolling membership' type group – it operates at the time of writing (that is April 2005). There is no fixed membership because, in a busy cardiac rehabilitation unit, there is a constant intake of people in recovery from a heart attack who have to be absorbed. The group meets twice each week for a whole afternoon. The composition is of mixed gender. Selection is partly based on physical criteria since the group spends the first part of an attendance working on essential exercise training under the direction of a physiotherapist. Those attending have to be capable of doing this without the risk of further damage to the heart. The rehabilitation nurse, physiotherapist and occupational therapist who jointly lead the group also bear in mind the need for members to be capable of fitting in with the education and support work and make individual provision for those who may not be able to cope.

The meetings follow a flexible pattern but normally after greetings, health checks and blood pressure assessments the ten or so members settle down to an hour of graded exercise training followed by 15 minutes of re-laxation. At this point the atmosphere changes and the members join to-gether for group work. These sessions sometimes have an educational input from a visitor. For example, the clinical psychologist may talk for a while on how stress affects the heart and teach approaches to identifying and mana-ging stress. Time is then given for the members to react to such material and reflect with one another on the aspects which apply to them and the im-plications for their current post-coronary phase of life. Other days there is no structure provided other than the nurse, occupational therapist or psychol-ogist invite the members to talk of how they are, the problems they are facing, their feelings as they grapple with the realities of a heart attack and the objectives they are pursuing. Naturally, much time is given to sharing per-sonal history and feeling and updating members on progress. The style of leadership is one of limited intervention, that is, allowing things to take their course and giving the group freedom to deal with issues of the day. However, groups of this type often invest heavily in a defensive jocularity, avoiding the task of the group. In such circumstances, whoever is leading the group does take a more active line in trying to settle the atmosphere and lead the members into addressing the important issues. (Do note, however, that hu-mour, laughter and 'unwinding' are important in a group of stressed people. Intervention is needed only when it becomes excessive and prolonged, thus becoming obstructive.)

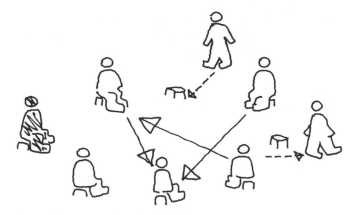

Figure 8 Open groups – people join and leave

In many ways this is the simplest of groups, functioning as an 'open group'. The targets are clear and the members are usually well motivated to participate. There is no fixed 'life' to the group, people join when a place is available and leave when they have made good progress physically and re-covered their confidence. The pay-off for the membership is abundantly clear and very similar to that of the pain group described in Chapter 1. People who have experienced the stress and fright of a heart attack often lose their way in life. They benefit from meeting with the other members and staff in the group because this breaks the isolation. The members become mutual sources of comfort and encouragement and the programme for the group gives general direction. The staff add to the feeling of increased security by being available to give personal advice. A final benefit comes from the sense of accountability that the group atmosphere promotes. Members are encouraged to plan ahead, declare objectives and specify targets for change. Naturally, progress in pursuing such goals is reported back to the group, hence there is an account-ability to the group. It can have the effect of an 'external conscience'. However, it is not always so simple. A heart attack can precipitate major psychological reactions, producing depression, anxiety or behaviour dis-turbance. Obviously when people attend a group they bring along whatever is in their head and sometimes this can be very difficult material. Similarly, the group may have to deal with the death of one of the members. Because a group of this type has no fixed membership, cohesion may vary from meeting to meeting and the sense of safety and trust which goes with it may also ebb and flow accordingly. The leaders have to take this into account and allow the membership at any one time to set the limits as to how much personal openness there can be, and what can or cannot be dealt with. Much is gov-erned by the trust that the members have in the people who lead the group. When that trust is strong, a great deal of useful ground can be covered, including even grief work, but nothing can or should ever be 'pushed' by the leaders. Gentle exploration and a great sensitivity to levels of safety are the order for this particular group situation.

Example 2 A support group for the partners of stroke victims

In Chapter 1 we touched briefly on the case of a woman whose husband had suffered a succession of small strokes. She had been a member of a 'stroke partners' group. This example relates the origins of this group.

A speech and language therapist worked for some years assisting people who had sustained a stroke and consequently lost their speech function. Her work gave her a degree of contact with the husbands and wives of those undergoing speech retraining. From the experiences related by these people she developed a view of the typical pattern of life once the stroke victim was home. She found herself in accord with the commonly reported finding that the partners of stroke victims often have a difficult time. If the damage from the stroke is severe, then there is considerable physical effort involved in giving care. Furthermore, the loss or gross deterioration of speech function places the partner in an exacting role which demands much patience and tolerance to strain as the one who has lost speech struggles to communicate, or uses the partner as a means of communicating with others.

As mentioned earlier, people who are thrust into the role of care-givers for the disabled often follow a similar path. The initial horror at the medical disaster leads them into a pattern of intense caring. Although well meant, this can foster an unnecessary dependency and lock the disabled person into the invalid role. Later, as the dependency becomes semi-permanent, life narrows for both the 'invalid' and the care-giver. This may well (although not always) provoke a deep resentment in the carer at the loss of freedom. It is expressed as the angry feeling that 'he no longer makes any effort at all, just expects me to do everything'. Life can become totally centred on the disability such that the partner leads a life that is virtually as restricted as that of the disabled person.

Such a situation is very complex psychologically. For some it leads to a tangle of resentment, anger and frustration mixed with the reciprocal feelings of guilt, compassion and hope. The confusion of feelings can be made much worse if the person involved is isolated in the sense of having no opportunity or 'permission' to express these feelings to an understanding support figure. Quite often the partner is put under pressure by the general practitioner and hospital staff to keep going as a co-opted medical auxiliary.

In the judgement of the speech therapist, the concern she felt for the partners took her to a level of involvement that went, perhaps, beyond the specific brief of her job. She was employed to give therapy to people with speech difficulties. She did not receive referrals to work with the partners of these people. However, after discussions with an advisor from the local clinical psychology service, she proposed to her head of department that a monthly support group be set up for the partners of those people who were receiving speech therapy after a stroke. The rationale for this group comprised two arguments. First, the group would help to maintain the morale and interest of the care-givers. Thus they would be much more likely to play a positive role as assistants in the disciplines and exercises of speech therapy which needed to be gone through each day. At the same time the partners would be able to exchange information and discuss difficulties, strategies for coping, and so on. In other words, the group facilitated informal mutual tuition and support.

Second, the speech therapist realized that she and the rest of her colleagues were in an unacceptable position. They, like the other services involved, contributed to the burdens of the partners by exerting a collusive pressure which permanently trapped the partner into a care-giving role. At the same time they offered no preparation, guidance or support. Consequently a proportion of these people themselves became 'patients' of one sort or another because of the stress. This, the speech therapist could see, was a contradiction in health care. Within the limited facilities of her department the introduction of a support group seemed the best way of eliminating this contradiction.

Again, the situation was that of a professional member of a health-care team who recognized the need for a support group but had no training in the group approach herself. However, she took advice, borrowed some literature and, keeping close contact with a clinical psychologist advisor, she planned the beginnings of her group.

As in the previous example, this was a group with the simple objectives of providing support, giving an opportunity for sharing and discussion, and reducing isolation (we use the word 'simple' in the sense that the group had no sophisticated targets such as personal learning, or studying group dynamics. However, simple though it might be, a group like this can have a major impact and become a turning point in people's lives.) The speech therapist elected for monthly meetings which were offered to partners whom she met at the speech clinic. There was no special selection policy, an offer of membership to the group being given on a routine basis as cases passed through the speech therapy department. Not all partners chose to join the group, thus numbers remained manageable, averaging at about eight to ten. The contract was straightforward. Members were invited to attend on the basis that they would review their experiences together and talk of how they were, the general atmosphere of their life and what objectives they were seeking to achieve. As the months passed they would follow each other's experiences through on the basis that, as care-givers, some form of care for themselves was essential. The group was to provide some, at least, of this care through a common effort at mutual understanding and support and the exchange of information and 'know how'. The group proved a success and settled down to a steady and unremarkable life. It worked out to be two-thirds or more women, with members tending to maintain their attendances for about six months on average.

A group like this can fluctuate greatly in mood from meeting to meeting. Sometimes the atmosphere was giggly and defensive, more akin to a coffee morning than a working group. The speech therapist was initially alarmed by this and saw it as a failing on her part. However, as the months passed she became more experienced in sensing how to lead the members into a more productive type of exchange. The brief transcript which follows illustrates this well. Eight members were in attendance and one of these, the wife of a 52-year-old man who had collapsed with a stroke three months before, was talking in a very superficial and defensive way about her feeling towards her husband.

> *Wife*:   Well, I can tell you that last week wasn't much fun. He had a couple of bad days and could barely talk at all, he seemed to be back right where he started. I know that he gets frustrated but he takes it out on me. Still, you know me, don't let it get you down is my motto. I just try and have a laugh about it to myself.

This was an important moment – an indication of distress is being given and then obscured by a coping process based on denial – the group picked up on the denying approach and began to share stories in the same vein. There was much laughter.

> *Member 1*:   When John gets like that I make faces at him behind his back. He caught me at it once (*laughter*) – well, I'd had enough for one day.
> *Member 2*:   Do you ever feel like just walking off for a day?
> *Member 3*:   More like a week. (*laughter*)
> *Wife*:   Now, now. (*turns to group leader*) Looks like I've started something, Rachael, it's more like a revolutionary group than a support group. What will you do with us?
> *Member 3*:   Oh, well, it does you good to have a laugh about it.
> *Wife*:   Yes, that's my philosophy, if you can turn it into a giggle, then you can keep going. If you stop and think about it – well, enough said. (*more laughter*)

It was this kind of exchange which worried Rachael, the speech therapist. She realized that it was just an evasion and that the sharing of important experiences and feelings was being displaced by defensive triviality. Her intervention saved the day, however.

> *Leader:*   I'd like to say something here if I may, OK? (*murmured consent*) I know that it does help to joke about these things but we would be dishonest with each other if we just gloss over this problem as a joke. Sarah, could you tell us a little more about bad days and what effect they have on you?
>
> *Sarah:*   (*After a long pause during which the group had fallen silent*) Alright, I'm going to tell you something which I've never said to anybody. You will all probably think I'm dreadful for saying this. I've always loved Peter, we got on very well. I still do love him really. But lately if I'm tired and if he is being difficult I sort of – can't feel my love. I almost hate him and I wonder how much longer it has to go on for – which is terrible and you have every right to be disgusted with me, especially you Rachael, after all your efforts.
>
> *Leader:*   Thanks for being so honest, Sarah. I wonder, how do we react to what she has said to us. I know that I understand perfectly and do not feel at all critical. It is very human to feel in two minds like this, particularly when people have changed so much.

Again there is a long pause, the mood of the group has totally changed, it has become reflective and charged with a sense of serious concern.

> *Member 1:*   I think that Sarah has been more honest than any of us. My feelings swing all over the place. I know exactly what she means. It's a relief to hear her say it because I've felt very ashamed at times. The vicar and church members come round and say how marvellous I am, what a tower of strength and all that, but they have no idea. On one awful day I felt so trapped and so lonely that I went up to my room and cried my heart out and I wished him dead.

During the ensuing half an hour the group functioned at a depth and intensity which both delighted and surprised the leader. Her intervention had effectively 'given permission' to the group to share secret feelings. With this came a collective awareness that the joking was over for a while and so the atmosphere changed to one of intimacy. Important things were said and thus important work was done. At a later meeting the members indicated that on the occasion just described they left the meeting feeling supported and more able to be honest about their own needs.

Clearly, this type of group has many applications wherever long-term home-based care is required. There is a vast array of literature which demonstrates that care-givers supporting mentally or physically handicapped people or those dealing with progressive neurological disorder, head injury, spinal injury, amputation or major disabling illnesses often do suffer stress and isolation and do need support. Thus if your work takes you into contact with people in this type of situation you might well consider creating a support group to help them through.

Example 3 Support groups for professional people

We will use several examples to illustrate this vast field of use.

Palliative care nurses

Specializing in work with dying people has many rewards. If, however, the psychological care element is properly done, then, it can also be very demanding work and a source of covert stress. A ward sister related her experiences to us following the eventual death of a 30-year-old man who died of cystic fibrosis on her ward. She spent many hours with this man and his young wife, helping them face his approaching death and the inevitable mountain of distressed feelings that accompany a premature death of this type.

The sister's experiences are instructive. She worked on her own in supporting the couple. This was primarily because she did not wish to stress the younger nurses, some of whom were trainees. Similarly she did not feel that she could draw on the help of her co-sister who had equal burdens. As a result she became isolated with the situation (the now familiar common ingredient to many of these scenarios you will note). She absorbed the emotions. She became caught up in the grief. She exhausted herself in comforting her patient and in her efforts to create a situation which would allow a death free from panic and despair. At one point she felt so stretched by this that she judged herself to be near some kind of breakdown. At the end of a day her needs were to be on her own, to be quiet and to take time out. However, in reality she had to go home and arbitrate in family disputes about which channel to have on the television, what to have for dinner, and so on. Consequently she was constantly irritable with the family and on some nights was withdrawn and tearful. She realized that this was unacceptable since she was imposing onto her own children or husband emotional reactions that belonged elsewhere. Her big mistake in all this was to work alone without regular supportive contact with colleagues. The importance of such contact was mentioned in Chapter 1. In her situation she needed to increase her efforts at self-care, mainly through the medium of support. In fact, she unwittingly set up the opposite, namely a regime of self-neglect.

Fortunately the sister responded to advice and linked up with a support group run for local hospice nurses. This involved a network arrangement whereby members could (and would) contact one another if they felt a need to work on troublesome issues, in which case the tendency was to meet as a pair. This was combined with a regular monthly meeting of the combined group. The meeting was led by a clinical tutor and had a fixed membership of 11 nurses, all of whom were women. They had all accepted an explicit contract. This simply involved an agreement to review with each other how they were feeling, and what experiences they had been through since last meeting. The emphasis was on sharing the emotions felt and the burdens carried in as open and honest a manner as possible.

Because the membership was stable, the level of group cohesion was high. That is, the members felt a strong sense of belonging. Thus, attendance at a meeting was usually an uplifting event with feelings of friendship and mutual support very much in evidence. Most times the individual members looked forward to the meetings and recognized the importance of reviewing their working and emotional experience with trusted colleagues. The meetings also provided opportunities for personal learning in terms of increased understanding about the nature of the circumstances that caused distress to individual members. Similarly it allowed members to learn from each other's experiences and to incorporate new attitudes and practices into their ways. The sister fitted in well with the group although she was not solely involved in terminal care nursing. The sense of strength which she drew from the group enabled her to continue with further arduous case work without such personal stress and distress.

A support group for school and college counsellors

A typical working day for a professional counsellor will involve five or six sessions with various types of clients each of an hour in length. Although the nature of the problems presented in the sessions will vary greatly, they will all have one thing in common. The clients will be presenting the counsellor with their distress, problems, conflicts and blocks to change, together with their sense of dependent expectation of help. Sometimes the burden of responsibility can be great, as in the case of child sexual abuse or students forewarning of suicide.

Some years ago Freudenberger (1974) introduced the term 'burn-out' to the literature of counselling and psychology. Later, other workers in the field extended our knowledge of the phenomenon and in particular Cherniss (1980) pressed the notion of burn-out as a threat to the health, psychological well-being and work effectiveness in the human services (that is professions such as counselling, social worker, nursing, teaching, and so on). In short, the long-term exposure to the demands of a job like counselling can bring about changes in which emotional exhaustion, the stereotyping of clients, and a reduced sense of personal worth in the role of counsellor undermine morale and lead to increasing stress and unhappiness.

In order to avert the onset of such problems the provision of long-term mutual supervision and support has steadily become more important to the counselling movement. It is of special relevance to us that, as in the last example, the group approach is perceived as an effective means of making this required support and mutual supervision available. It is powerful in its effect and economic in terms of time consumption. Both authors have been members of such a group which has been in existence for over 20 years. The group meets about once a month during the school and college terms and has a fairly stable membership of about seven counsellors. The usual format (after tea and greetings) is for each counsellor to take several minutes to make contact with the feelings which they are bringing to the group. This is an attempt to try to slow down from the usual pace of work and life and ask the question 'What feelings are predominant in me, what are they related to, and what else can be detected near the surface which has been masked by the usual pressures of a busy life?' The members thus report their state of feeling to the group. These are by no means always negative feelings, it should be said. People have ups as well as downs and it is normal for some of the group to be feeling robust and confident, others 'OK' but tired, and sometimes a couple will have run into something which has disturbed them.

The group has a contract which entrusts members, on identifying significant problems and emotional upheaval, to accept the responsibility to ask for some group time and work through the issue in detail. The members trust each other deeply. Group cohesion and mutual support are strong. Thus, with a gentle leadership which is always slanted towards maintaining a caring and supportive atmosphere, the group has managed to deal with a wide range of personal issues. Some of these have been about difficulties in the counselling role such as excessive work pressure, the failure of management and other staff to understand the role properly, troublesome cases and perturbing career problems. At other times it has dealt with grief following a death, personal relationships in trouble and the impact of personal illness. Behind all this there is the notion that a counsellor or psychological therapist must practise self-care and must also monitor and work on personal feelings which influence the way they deal with clients. This support group proves very effective indeed in achieving such objectives. The authors recommend the approach to any body of professional people engaged in care-giving work.

Support groups for NHS managers

A community health trust that had served the whole of an English county for many years was to be broken up and reformed into more localised primary care health trusts and one separate mental health trust. Some of the senior managers in the original trust were to be made redundant while all the others had to apply for jobs within the new trusts. It was a difficult and unpleasant time for some of them, hence one of the authors was contacted and requested to offer a support group facility. The group met monthly for slightly longer than a year and then the membership was split because of the closure of the original trust. In a follow-up evaluation it became known that, in general, the members had appreciated the group and found that it had been a help in fostering better communication and understanding between the members and had offered true support during difficult times. Based on this, another sector of managers from the new trusts let it be known that they felt in need of something similar because their current roles were exceptionally pressured and stressing. They also had to deal with the continuing culture of change within their trusts which meant that their roles were subject to threat and instability. This group ran for two years and again was well appreciated. The monthly meetings were a time for review, the sharing of circumstances of upheaval and stress together with an hour or so of valued supportive companionship.

Personal learning and support groups for trainee GPs

In comparatively recent times, the profession of general medical practitioner has come to be recognized as a specialism within medicine. Young doctors wishing to become GPs must undertake special postgraduate training over a period of some three years. This training is aimed at introducing them to necessary new skills, developing further their existing professional and interpersonal skills, and supporting them during what is often a difficult period of transition. Different parts of the country have developed varying vocational training schemes. One scheme we know well increased its investment in small group work with doctors. Having tried out several formats, the organizers ran a number of groups with about nine or ten members in each, meeting weekly for an hour and a quarter. While not yet fully qualified GPs, the members were all fully qualified doctors, often with wide experience and hospital specialist expertise. Some, in their final year of training, would be already acting as full members of a medical practice in the community, with their own patients, regular surgeries, and all the usual duties.

These groups have much in common with those described earlier, and similar benefits were derived by many. However, some of the doctors found the group experience difficult to come to terms with after their earlier medical training. Several doctors found that the groups helped them to deal with the demands of their new role and become confident and less isolated in tackling the considerable difficulties they encountered. It was often a great relief for individuals to discover they were not the only one in the group to find the going rough, and to be able to share their experiences in a protected setting.

Case study A young doctor's experience

As an example, one young doctor shared with the group the experience of having a terminally ill elderly patient die shortly after having received a pain-killing injection. The family and the doctor were present. It was clear that the doctor had acted impeccably, but still needed to digest the sequence of events, and look after personal emotion touched by the occasion. As with other helping groups, the members were able to offer needed support, and to benefit themselves not only by being effective care-givers, but by feeling their own way through the episode with their colleague, and thus gain understanding and control of their own material.

While these groups functioned very well as support groups, the members sometimes expressed confusion at 'not having been taught anything'. These difficulties probably resulted from expectations formed during medical training by exposure to a manner of instruction that taught 'correct' practice from wrong, and in some ways required the doctor to act as a technically perfect automaton. As a result young doctors could easily feel insecure in situations where there is no obvious 'right way'. Thus the groups give many opportunities to become accustomed to new ways of learning. The doctors could wonder aloud about perplexing cases, generate alternatives, consider different ways of reacting to and dealing with patients, free from the burden of being thought 'weak' for having doubts. It was thus possible to learn new styles of thinking and relating rather than being fed facts. The full value of the learning in the group often became apparent later. As the trainees became more experienced in fulfilling the role of GP, it was possible to appreciate more fully the benefit to themselves and their patients of the very human qualities they had explored in the groups.

Here is a brief extract from another group, this time for experienced GPs, which illustrates something of the process at work. The extract has been modified slightly to ensure total anonymity, but does represent an actual exchange. Doctor A has been talking about the difficulty of coping with an overly-friendly patient:

> *Doctor A:*   I knew I had to make contact with her again. I had very mixed feelings. There was a very real problem for me in that she had trespassed too far. We talked about it, and she obviously hadn't heard what I was saying, hadn't wanted to hear that there was a very real problem. So, while I was ashamed of my behaviour that morning, and could certainly say 'I'm sorry you feel hurt', I felt I couldn't hide behind excuses and pretend that there wasn't a real problem. Yet to talk that over with her was going to be very painful too.

Leader: It wasn't just that you were brusque in treating her then, as you said earlier?

Doctor A: No. It wasn't, that was neither here nor there, in a sense.

Doctor B: It looks as if whatever you do, she's going to feel hurt.

Doctor A: Yes, that's right.

Doctor B: In fact, that's the way she's designed the drama.

Doctor A: Now I think of it, looking back over her life, it's part of her make-up.

Leader: I wonder if we could pause there? I'm sure that's hooking all kinds of things for us. Does anyone else want to respond to the story so far?

All the group members took part, and helped the presenting doctor explore and understand all the difficulties, and to think of how to manage things more successfully.

Like other helping professionals, doctors are often subject to considerable pressure from the demands made on them by working with the personal distress of their patients. In common with other helpers too, they often seem remiss in seeing to their own personal emotional maintenance. Some doctors are even offended at any suggestion that they might have a need for such care, taking it as a sign of 'weakness' and 'unprofessional'. The authors remain convinced that such support is of great importance, and if adopted as a matter of routine might well result in fewer casualties among doctors. We would like to see doctors as a matter of course developing the habit of using a proper support group as a routine part of their professional practice. Jenkinson and Smerdon (1988) give a fuller account of the development of these groups.

Support groups in secondary education

Successive governments in recent years have continually sought to improve the quality of our educational system. The result has been a continuous stream of initiatives of one kind or another so that change has been endemic. Consequently, both teachers and pupils have had to come to terms with a rapidly changing landscape, including the National Curriculum, re-modelled assessment tests, the ever-present performance targets, the demands of new technology, and wide changes in society. It could be argued that the need for some kind of extra support within the school system has never been greater. The small support group approach has much to commend it.

Case study A support group for pupils
The door, which had been standing very slightly ajar, flies open, and in storms a very angry young woman. To the small group of assorted pupils in the room already she exclaims 'That bloody woman!' This is received quietly by the group,

and by the school counsellor acting as leader. They shuffle along to make room for her. She flings herself down on a chair in dramatic fashion, and glares around. After a while, with gentle prompting, the story emerges that she has just rushed out of a lesson by a teacher with whom she has been having a running dispute, being convinced she is being 'picked on' and generally victimized. After the first eruption in the group, the other members, ranging from 11 to 15 years old, begin to discover the developments behind this, and eventually to invite her to consider how she might have herself contributed to the crisis. The counsellor has to be ultra careful, as he is aware that the girl has been undergoing intensive personal therapy, working through traumatic events in her family, and is under considerable pressure. He must safeguard the girl's confidential personal material, while also enabling her to consider her outburst in relation to her personal life. He must avoid sympathetic collusion with the girl, for instance, by siding with her against the teacher. Equally, he must avoid out-of-hand condemnation of the girl's behaviour. By and by, the girl composes herself, announces that she is now ready to go back and 'face the music', knowing full well that she has been out of order, and departs.

This group took place in a large comprehensive school in the Home Counties, and was run on somewhat unusual lines. The 'group contract' between the counsellor and his clients was that if his door was firmly closed, then a confidential personal counselling session was taking place and was not to be interrupted, short of dire emergency. At other times, and between certain pre-arranged hours, all were welcome according to need. Great trust was invested both by the school staff, and by the pupils, and (amazingly perhaps) the integrity of the system was respected. In the end, there were no losers. A very high degree of skill was shown by the counsellor, but also by the children, often formerly seen as 'troublemakers', 'attention seekers', and 'misfits', in learning to use appropriately the resource the group represented, eventually returning to normal school life.

The counsellor concerned had an additional resource, in that a second adult was present, a trainee counsellor taking a postgraduate advanced diploma course, on placement at the school. Though a trainee in counselling terms, the student was very experienced in group work, and was also a quite senior member of staff in a well-respected school distantly situated in the same county. As such he had the ear of senior staff in the comprehensive school, some of whom were at the very least ambivalent about the recent arrival of a specialist school counsellor. He was able to explain aspects of the new service while safe-guarding confidentiality and, consequently, relations between the counsellor and staff improved. Both counsellor and trainee were able to offer insight into the behaviour and professional practice of the other, with special reference to the group described, and were able to review events together in a non-threatening, non- blaming, but challenging and creative way.

Case study A support group for school staff

At a different school, a middle-ranking male member of staff conceived the idea of trying out an informal group for staff. Originally the group had no agenda other than to compare notes and let off some of the steam generated in the working week. He was agreeably surprised to find that not only did colleagues turn up, they were very forthcoming about the difficulties they were experiencing. They in turn were surprised to find that difficulties they thought were the result of their own individual failings were also being experienced by others. As some of the members were very senior indeed, and widely respected in the school by staff and pupils alike, as good teachers and disciplinarians, it was a revelation to the newly qualified teachers, and gave them great support and encouragement. All were able eventually to look at how they might be themselves contributing to their own difficulties, and find new ways of handling troublesome situations. Most importantly, they found they could do this without feeling ashamed and defensive, nor condemning the children who were making their lives so difficult.

The young teacher running the group was fortunate to be able to get supervision as he was in contact with a large group-training establishment. He was there able to discover and come to terms with his own welter of feelings at (as he saw it) his own temerity in taking on such a task. In particular, it was very difficult to accord all group members equal status, as quite clearly within the school power hierarchy, some were more equal than others. But in terms of being tested by the children, exhaustion, and other compelling matters, all were equal, and one person's experience was as valid as another. As a by-product of this group, communication within the staff was improved, tension eased, and most importantly the treatment of the admittedly difficult children improved.

Support groups in industry and commerce

In some ways support groups in the industrial and commercial settings are a rather more difficult venture and probably less appropriate for a beginner in leading support groups. A staff under stress that needs support is often hostile to its management and thus there is a 'political' context that has to be taken into account. For example, in the era of 'downsizing' following the privatization of many state-owned British industries, it was common to find staff at most levels working under sustained pressure and discomfort as a result of reduced staffing levels. One of the authors was approached for advice concerning support group facilities in such an organization. However, it did not seem a suitable context at the time since the management were, in fact, looking for a means to improve the tolerance of the staff to stress and so reduce sick leave while maintaining heavy pressure on their staff. The staff, on the other hand, were alienated from management, perceiving them as the source of their difficulties by means of unreasonable demands. It was judged likely that an open support group would fail if management made up some of the group while at the same time the management were suspicious of there being a closed group of service staff only – fearing a low key subversive effect. No support group was formed. Similarly support groups among staff who compete against one another for commission or rewards for best sales figures can be a venture destined to end in difficulty and failure.

It is not always the case though and in settings where there is a degree of cooperative harmony in a staff that is pulling together, successful support groups can flourish and be a useful facet of company life.

Case study A support group for training staff in a large financial firm
The training department in a large firm had suffered a trauma with the death of two colleagues in a car crash. A member of staff in the personnel department had received some training in counselling and support group work and so she offered to run a couple of support group meetings for the staff to help them come to terms with the deaths. These meetings were found to be helpful and it was agreed that they should continue on a once-a-month basis as a general support group. As the group matured, members discussed difficulties in their work (mainly to do with running courses and handling 'difficult' delegates) and sometimes issues to do with wider aspects of their lives. It was a successful group and lasted until the firm was involved in a merger.

In general terms, presenting the case for support group work within industry and commerce is more difficult than with, say, health-care professionals. Nevertheless many people can accept the point that to engage in a high demand/high stress role without an effort at self-care can eventually lead to a deterioration in physical and mental health. A corollary to this is that to hold authority or management responsibility over those in a high demand/high stress role brings with it a duty of care and therefore an obligation to provide some way of monitoring staff well-being and providing protective measures. The support group is an obvious option in relation to both of these points, especially in view of the opportunity for *self-monitoring* that membership in a support group provides. Figure 9 serves well as an overview of the function of support groups in presentations to a critical audience where a convincing rationale is called for. The emphasis on self-monitoring forms the basis of the argument.

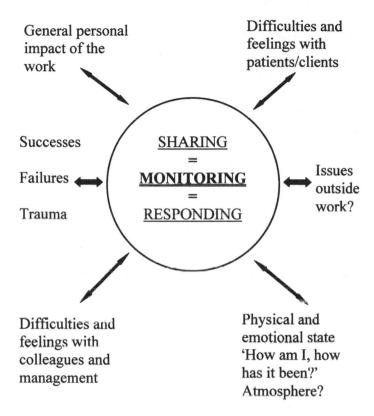

General personal
impact of the
work

Difficulties and
feelings with
patients/clients

Successes

Failures

Trauma

SHARING
=
MONITORING
=
RESPONDING

Issues
outside
work?

Difficulties and
feelings with
colleagues and
management

Physical and
emotional state
'How am I, how
has it been'?'
Atmosphere?

Figure 9 The work of a support group

3 Preparation 2
The group leader

If you are contemplating establishing a helping group, it is appropriate that you will have in mind several questions regarding your suitability as a leader. This chapter poses a few such questions on your behalf. Note, though, that because there is so little truly reliable research into such issues, we will base the discussion on a personal rather than an academic viewpoint. This means that we will be using our own observations and experience, underpinned by our own training and reading, as a basis for our recommendations.

Does a group leader need to be a special kind of person?

While we believe it is true that a leader does require certain values, beliefs, skills and understanding to be effective, it is also true that these usually can be acquired. You do not have to be a 'born leader' to succeed. In fact, some of the behaviours thought of as desirable in a natural leader actually may be counter-productive in a support group. For instance, a firm insistence that one's own view is the only correct one, and that it should be adopted by all others in the group, is unlikely to be helpful. Similarly, a tendency to take control and dominate a group is likely to be unproductive in the long run. This takes us to a key statement:

> The manner in which you set up and run a group is very important. The kind of person you are as a leader will be assessed by the group based on how they see you acting, what you do and say and the timing and manner of your delivery. Conclusions will be drawn and inferences made, based largely on your behaviour. This will have great significance because members who have no group experience inevitably will be searching for a 'role model', that is, an example of the behaviour required in a group. You need to give the appropriate example.

Do not be put off by this statement because it is really a statement of the obvious and something that most of us live with in one way or another for much of our working lives. There is likely to be some variation between people who work with groups as to the ideal profile for a group leader. We set out below our own preferred version, organized under headings that reflect different aspects of human functioning.

Key beliefs and values

Groups are about change and thus those involved in leading them need to value and understand the nature of personal change. Implicit in the notion of a training group and, to a lesser degree, the support group, is the core belief that people have a continuing ability to learn, change and grow psychologically, if they are so motivated. As many of the significant personality theorists argue, we must always see people as permanently engaged in the 'process of becoming', for example, Kelly (1955) and Rogers (1961). It is a generous idea and suggests that people can be continually open to revising their views about how the world is and their views of themselves in it. Since group work evolved with the objective of finding ways to facilitate growth and change, there is little point in people using the technique unless they place high value on such objectives. In short, *group leaders must value personal change and growth.*

   Similarly, the expansion of group technique has taken place with the assumption that the relief of psychological pain, distress and discomfort is also a central, valued objective. Comfort is not, though, an objective which obliterates all other considerations. According to circumstances, the truly effective leader will tolerate 'constructive emotional pain' as a means to growth. In other words, group meetings are not just warm, syrupy chat sessions, but places to conduct discussion which, although perhaps painful at the time, leads on to positive change and growth. For example, it may be that a support group is having difficulty facing something unpleasant such as grief or anger. Sooner or later it will be necessary to go through the discomfort involved in members being open and dealing with their feelings in order to free the group from defensive avoidance. Here, then, are two more essential values, *the pursuit of ultimate psychological peace combined with a recognition of the benefits of 'constructive emotional pain'.*

Openness to emotion and personal feelings

It is of prime importance that people who lead groups value that part of human functioning which we call feelings. The concept of feelings is, incidentally, rather more complicated than that of emotion. Whereas one might have periods without any particularly heightened emotion, one can never be without feeling, since by this we mean the current physical and psychological stance of the person. As you read this, you cannot be without feeling and if you do not know what that feeling is, simply study the general 'atmosphere' of your body. It may tell you that you are relaxed and absorbed, physically ill at ease and fidgety because you are in a hurry or struggling to concentrate, exasperated because you want to hear how to run a group without all these considerations, etc. If you want to know how you feel, ask your body and relate this to your awareness of what is going on at any one moment. Sometimes our body state can reveal that we are in a feeling state for which we had no conscious recognition at the time, i.e. *identifying the atmosphere of our body can help to 'surface' feelings.*

This facility for awareness of feelings is essential for those intending to lead groups, not the least reason being that the aim of most groups is to promote the discovery, expression and sharing of feelings. Clearly, if the leader has difficulty in working with feelings, then this is a major handicap for a group. Because of this, it is better if intending leaders become members of a simple training and personal learning group to develop these abilities before taking on leadership. However, we have already acknowledged that quite often this proves impossible, in which case you can do some personal work on your own and you will find Gendlin (1978) a useful aid. He offers a written guide to a technique called 'focusing' which is designed to help people develop ready access to their own feeling life.

As a final word on this theme, we should be quite explicit and answer the question 'How does one know if such personal development work needs to be undertaken?' If you can give a 'yes' to the following items which are put together as a checklist, then you have already made considerable progress in your personal growth. If you find yourself saying 'no', then you must face the reality that if you are about to start a group, you will do so without, in our view, one of the more important assets. In this case, some preparatory work with a counsellor or clinical psychologist, or time in a group as a member yourself, is recommended:

- Do you know that you are aware of and open to the flow of personal feelings in your daily life – do others confirm this to be so?
- Are you able to say that you value your own feelings and allow their expression rather than striving to mask them?
- Are you able to share your feelings with a trusted companion without being defensive?
- Are you able to receive and experience the feelings of others in a relaxed, accepting manner without wanting immediately to placate, soothe or distract them from expressing feeling?
- Do you judge that if a person expresses or 'acts out' feeling in a group you will be able to allow this to unfold without a panicky need to take control and return to more matter-of-fact issues?

What kind of skills and understanding will I need as a support group leader?

Perhaps we can consider this through the reflections of one particular person who asked for supervision in setting up a group. Paula, a nurse, had already been a member in several different groups, and had already tried her hand as a leader. She was about to start leading a support group for colleagues working in her hospital. The following conversation was with her supervisor while in a tutorial with other nurses curious about group work:

Supervisor: I expect you've put quite a lot of thought into this group. I wonder why you're taking on this commitment, what you expect to get out of it?

Paula: It's a good question, and I wonder myself sometimes. I think I've got something useful to offer and it seems like a worthwhile enterprise. I feel that there's not enough provision for support and I want to help. There's a lot that people can do for each other in a group, if only I can get them together and helping each other.

Supervisor: Is there anything else you expect to get out of it personally?

Paula: I suppose there is, really. If this goes well, I might be able to establish a few more groups, and that would be interesting. As it is, perhaps I'll come to be known as a good group leader, and meanwhile I'll be getting useful experience.

Supervisor: So this might be the start of something for you?

Paula: Yes, it's a logical development of what I've done so far.

Supervisor: How about inside the group, while you're running it?

Paula: How do you mean?

Supervisor: Well, you've spoken about external pay-offs for your work. Are there any that you expect while actually working with the group, from the group itself?

Paula: That's hard for me to say at the moment. I hope they'll develop a respect for me as a group leader. Maybe they'll be able to see things in a different light sometimes as a result of what I say, and that will be satisfying.

Supervisor: You'll be getting satisfaction from teaching them things?

Paula: Yes, but that's not quite what I meant. It's more that I'll be pleased if I feel I've been effective in helping them look freshly at old difficulties, at how observations and feelings in the past may have misled them into particular behaviours today. Even though they may be doing the hard work, maybe they wouldn't be able to do it without me and the group.

Supervisor: You aim to be a sort of catalyst, in whose presence reactions happen, and then to help the group learn from those reactions?

Paula: Yes, that's more the feel of it. It'll be my job to keep the work of the group firmly in our sights and to make sure we look after each other appropriately as well. But really, that's everybody's job. I'll just be in a good position to say if things are getting neglected or out of hand.

Supervisor: That makes you sound more like a detached observer, different from the rest. Is that how you see it?

Paula: In any group there are usually several issues running at once, sometimes at different levels. I have to try and keep track of them and not get stuck on one to the neglect of the others. If I do get stuck on one, I think in time someone else in the group will notice it and jog me on. But I certainly aim to spend a lot of time really listening to what's going on.

Supervisor: You make it sound quite demanding.

Paula: No, not really, I've spent a lot of time in groups run by other people and you get to notice patterns recurring, moods in the group, sets of behaviours, connections between things and reactions in yourself. Sometimes they belong to you but quite often they're much more to do with what's going on in the group. So you chance your arm a little, ask the group to consider what they have seen and why they think it has happened. Theory's useful too in helping you see what might be significant and in suggesting ways of behaving that you might find effective. I plan to keep reading books on groups and talking to you.

We can see from this exchange that Paula has given a good deal of thought to the kind of group she wishes to run and should have enough going for her to stand a good chance of running a really successful group. She clearly acknowledges her own motivation, seeming acceptably open to her own stake in the group's success, but not out to exploit the members for her own ends. Although, strictly speaking, she should have already thought through the questions put to her in this first interview, in addressing them there and then she proves capable of tracking her own feelings in response to the interviewer. Her comments on her own group experience show her to be mindful and aware of the feelings of others. She has a businesslike approach to the work of the group and concern for appropriate care within the group. She shows herself quite prepared to check observations and ideas with the group and is open to alternative suggestions from the members. Her past group history and intentions for the group augur well for a good atmosphere developing.

You will find that discussion among people involved in group work and also relevant literature often use the term 'group process'. We elaborate on this in Chapter 6. Basically, the notion is that groups tend to develop a particular theme to their manner of functioning and that the members (sometimes unwittingly) all play their part in this. For example, rather than overcome the awkwardness of talking about their own difficulties, members may sense that one person will accept copious attention and so turn that person into the 'group patient'. Thereafter much time may be devoted to discussion of his or her problems, thus allowing other members to avoid dealing with their own. A person in Paula's position, possibly yourself, that is, cannot be expected to develop instant expertise in recognizing such group process. Nevertheless, unless the group is to drift helplessly wherever it will, *some basic abilities in identifying and responding to patterns in a group need to be developed on the part of the leader.* We will review these under four headings:

1   **Observation of behaviour**: In plain English, as leader, you will need to keep your eyes and ears open, to 'take it all in'. You will need to give full attention, without being over-intense. It is usual for a leader to try and keep track of who is doing the most talking and who is not; who speaks when, for how long and how frequently, at whom do they look, etc.

    There are many more behaviours that it is useful to keep track of, some of which we will discuss later. For now, it is sufficient to establish that it is important to try and monitor the physical happenings in the group, and their timing.

2   **Making sense of theme: review, discussion and analysis**: In terms of the group process, the central question for you is 'what do I think is going on here?' In seeking to answer, it is as well to be cautious, especially when ascribing meaning to observed behaviour. The important thing is that you try to make sense of it but keep an open mind while doing so. Review and discussion with someone experienced in groups can be a very important asset if you can arrange it.

3   *Noting the focus of attention*: The question needs to be held firmly in mind as to whether the group is attending to its basic task. Instead, it may be off on some concern of its own, maybe avoiding difficult work by defensively 'labouring' at 'spoof' work. For instance, one group, faced with hard ground to cover became very interested in the physical characteristics of the room they were occupying and much time was expended on whether a new and better room was to be found, there and then. The room had been used many times before without comment. In fact, the real problem was that a member had walked out of group saying it was a waste of time because another of the members 'hogged the conversation'. This had created a great deal of tension.

4   **Note the emergence of norms and rules**: Whether group members realize it or not, there are bound to be values and norms of some kind within their group that influence their behaviour and participation. This applies to all groups, whether with experienced or inexperienced members. For example, in a newly formed support

group whose members have never taken part in group work before, there may be unspoken 'rules' relating to boundaries and limits, that is, notions of how far it is permissible to go in the group with personal disclosure. There may be taboo subjects, restrictions on being 'too personal', and so on. These rules are all about making a situation that initially feels unsafe rather more comfortable. You, as leader, need to be mindful of this tendency and stay watchful in order to detect clear patterns of approach and avoidance that could limit the usefulness of the group. That way you will gain insight into the identity of such 'rules' and be able to help the group to avoid becoming handicapped by them. Gently pointing them out and modelling alternatives would be the usual means of dealing with, say, a group situation where there are restrictive rules.

Even this brief list will appear awesome to an absolute beginner in group work – but it is not as difficult as it might sound. A survival kit for such a beginner, and one both authors use all the time, reads as follows:

- **Watch and listen carefully to what is going on – both within the members and yourself.**
- **Try to make sense of it in terms of something affecting all the members – a running theme in part or all of a meeting.**
- **Keep an open mind – do not allow yourself to become 'locked on to' a particular idea about the group theme, keep asking yourself if there are alternative explanations.**
- **Try to be clear just what it is you, as leader are trying to do at any one time.**
- **Discuss it with an experienced group leader at a later date.**

What will be my responsibilities as a support group leader?

Other than the administrative task of running the group, creating a membership, a working environment and time-keeping, the responsibilities have to do with communication, care and helping the group to be productive. The leader must ensure that the group members know what it is all about, that is, what the group is for and how they are expected to behave. Any ground rules for the group should be made explicit and agreed early on; matters such as confidentiality need to be tackled in a matter-of-fact way, so that people know where they are. Similarly, in a helping group, it is the leader's responsibility to intervene if anyone in the group appears to be significantly at risk. For instance, as suggested above, it is quite common for a group to become so interested in one member that their curiosity, or their need to 'solve' the problems, leads them to ignore warning signals from the 'chosen one' that they have had enough. If the group persists unchecked in its efforts to help, the presenting member can quickly feel hounded and victimized. For its part, once the group realizes what it has done, the members can be frightened at their own power to cause distress when they were 'only trying to help', consequently suffering a setback and loss of confidence in their ability to help. Of course, by intervening, the leader becomes open to the charge of wanting to control and over-protect, of 'always interfering just when things were getting interesting'. We believe it is safer to err on the side of caution; after all, if the leader has, in fact, made a mistake and intervened protectively too early, the 'victim' can always say so and go further if it feels right.

In terms of overall objectives, the basic responsibility, however, is to establish, so far as it is within anyone's power, conditions conducive to support and, perhaps, beneficial change. *It is the leader's responsibility to make sure that the members feel safe and thus free to explore and work psychologically.* This safety is generated by the model of behaviour given by the leader, the terms of operation for the group set out by the leader, and the leader's ability to make people feel equally valued, worthwhile and supported.

Am I suitable to be a support group leader?

Almost certainly you will have detected the ambivalence in our position. We recognize that groups, even the simplest of support groups, have much to offer and thus we urge more people in the caring profession to use them. However, very few people in the professions have training and many within the field of group work would see the use of untrained leaders as a disaster. As you will have gathered, we do not. However, at the same time we do take a very carefully qualified position. Our point is that in order to make support groups more readily available, certain types of people, although untrained, should be encouraged to run basic support groups provided that they make the effort to become informed and link with a person who can act as an advisor/supervisor. We do not consider it a good idea for people to set up a group and 'do their own thing' without this sort of back-up. We should like to make it very clear that many people will prove unsuitable as group leaders, and this is not an invitation for all and sundry to 'have a go'. Give some thought to what we have written in this chapter and enquire about where you have got to in your personal awareness and development. If you have doubts, contact a local counsellor or clinical psychologist and examine the issue further with them. If, in all honesty, you feel a very different person from the profile that has emerged, our view is that you should *not* attempt to run a group. If you feel in accord with the objectives of groups and the key characteristics of group leaders as described above but are diffident about your strength in these, then proceed, but with caution. Accept that you may need to obtain some preparatory experiences and do turn to your local resources for help. If you start as an untrained leader you will probably feel unsure and hesitant (it would be worrisome if you did not), but the experience in your group will teach and shape you. We hope also to make a guiding contribution to your development through the pages of this book.

4   Preparation 1
The group members

When should the responsibilities of a group leader begin? We have no doubt that they begin the moment a person or set of people have been invited by a leader to join a group. We are quite emphatic about this point. This is because we have witnessed the impact that a lack of thoughtful pre-group preparation can sometimes have upon people who have agreed to join a group. The situation can be very disturbing, even damaging, because to those who are wholly uninformed about groups the anxious fantasy of what is to come can produce a nightmare version of the event. In such fantasies the group may be seen not as a place of care and support but a place with a threatening nature where one is put through some kind of ordeal and exposed to unpleasant experiences, such as 'being shown up', 'making a fool of myself', or 'breaking down when talking about it'.

The following conversation is taken from a tape-recorded therapy session and is reproduced exactly as it occurred. A psychologist is talking to a 34-year-old woman who has been attending weekly therapy sessions to do with her prevailing problems with anxiety.

Figure 10 What is to come?

Therapist: How has your week been – did you get any further with your plan to visit your sister?

Client: I didn't, no. (*long pause*) I've had a really bad week to be honest – really bad. In fact I very nearly phoned you Monday morning.

Therapist: Has something upset you, then?

Client: You will probably think it's silly. I've been worrying about this group that you said you hope I would start going to next week. It's been on my mind every day. I suppose I've got in a state about it, you know. At nights particularly – the dreams have been frightening. They leave me wound up and tense during the day.

Therapist: But, Cara, I thought you knew that the group is to help you. It's not a place where you will get hurt. I would never have suggested it otherwise. We talked about it last week and you seemed to take the suggestion of the group happily enough. What has happened meantime to upset you?

Client: Nothing has happened. I've just been thinking about it. It's not knowing what goes on, what I'm supposed to say or do. I remembered a play that was on the radio once. A lot of the story was about a group and – I don't know – they were all cruel to each other. I can't get it out of my mind. There's no way I could stay in a room with that kind of thing going on, even just being there would make me so anxious, I know, and if people started talking to me like that, I wouldn't be able to stay, it would be terrifying. I know that you are trying to help me – God knows what you think of me for being so weak – the truth is, I'm in such a state about it, I don't think that I'll be able to go. I didn't know how to tell you.

Therapist: You are not dealing with reality though. You know that I will be guiding the group and that the others in it will be people with much the same difficulty as you – you will be quite safe and well looked after.

Client: Maybe – well, alright, in a way I believe that. But it sort of took over, I spent half the night last Sunday sitting up worrying, I just felt so frightened about it, the thought of having to face ten people that I have never met is bad enough but being trapped in there and having to say personal things to them, or talk about my own feelings – I know it's stupid and I'm being ridiculous but it is the most frightening thing that I've had to face for a long while.

Therapist: I understand, let me try and explain things to you in more detail so that you will be more reassured.

The most obvious thing about this example is that it did not have to happen. In fact, being more direct, it never should have happened and was a clear example of negligence. The lessons and conclusions are straightforward. To the experienced leader a group is a place of great healing and helping potential, a place where fears are eased away. Not so for people who do not truly know what to expect and combine various social anxieties with false information or fearful images. Without careful and considered preparation, impending group members are exposed to the risk of unnecessary distress, as seen in the example above. Rarely does a group get through the first meeting without one or more of the members revealing that they are nervous and have worried during the lead-up to the day when the group began. Sometimes people can be the victims of fantasies so far from the realities of group life as to seem absurd. One young man had been silent and withdrawn throughout this first group meeting. Finally, he spoke up and confessed that he was very nearly sick during the opening half hour because he was convinced that he would be asked to stand up in front of a lectern and talk to the rest of the members and thus be judged by them. The absence of a lectern, the friendly circle of chairs and the easy-going atmosphere with the leader's invitation to talk only when one felt ready and confident were his first real understanding of the fact that his group, like all other helping groups, was a place of respite, not attack.

You, the intending leader, have a responsibility to head off such problems to as great an extent as is possible. You will never stop all pre-group anxieties, but you can modify or prevent those generated by false beliefs and insufficient information. But the task does not stop at limiting anxieties for, if the members have a persistently inaccurate idea of what they or the group leader are supposed to be doing, then the whole course of the group can be irretrievably deflected from the ideal path. In extreme cases a group can be rendered wholly ineffective as a result. Thus, good pre-group preparation is a very worthwhile investment of time and energy.

Understanding the problem and the reasons for pre-group preparation

The general topic of pre-group preparation has been reviewed by one of the authors in a separate journal article, Nichols (1976). Because we regard this as such an important issue we will briefly outline some of the key points and arguments given in that article. First, it has been established that three features of 'group life' are consistently related to a positive outcome for members. These are: (1) the development of group cohesion; (2) effective modelling by the leader or experienced members; and (3) pre-group preparation.

In the absence of efficient pre-group preparation cohesion may fail to develop. Any modelling which occurs may well be lost since a group without cohesion and a sense of safety will probably be in disarray. In short, *effective preparation for group membership acts as a foundation for other elements that control the success of group development.* The reasons are that the wholly unprepared member may bring into a group meeting certain disadvantages in the form of beliefs and attitudes which effectively block positive participation in the group and which, if acted out forcefully, may disrupt it completely. Nichols suggests that five such factors should be noted:

1   Obstructing misconceptions
2   Inappropriate role expectations
3   Distracting emotions
4   Defensive group dynamics
5   Poor motivation, acting-out, dropping-out.

Obstructing misconceptions

People will vary of course, but a good many of those who have received no pre-group preparation will, as shown above, be possessed of gross misconceptions concerning what goes on in a group and what part they have to play in it. The fears of being forced to make shameful revelations, of being exposed to scorn, or undergoing experiences which either embarrass or demand too much of a person are surprisingly common.

The issue of receiving help in a group setting is also likely to be misunderstood, particularly by people who have received individual support or therapy. It is easy for them to believe that group work is simply a diluted and inferior form of individual support. This can provoke feelings both prior to and during the group of being abandoned as a significant individual. Similarly, it may create needs to compete for attention which can disrupt the group cohesion. In the same way if a person already receiving some form of individual intervention transfers to a group with the belief that the objectives of the group are the same as those held in the individual work, this too is a serious misconception which will cause difficulties.

A final and very common misconception is a belief that causes trouble in both group and individual approaches. It is best captured in the phrase 'what's the use of talking about it?' When people arrive at a group believing that what they really need is some form of treatment or procedure to which they should be passive recipients, then a prolonged and usually unsatisfactory struggle ensues. Only when members of a group understand that it is what they bring to a group and express within it that generates the power of a group to help and to change will there be a positive outcome.

Inappropriate role expectations

Obviously if people arrive at a group with an inaccurate idea of what is to happen they are likely to adopt roles which are inappropriate. This is less so where the type of group offers in its name a guide to the activity. For example, the title Mastectomy Support Group suggests in itself that the event is about the discussion of the effect and experience of mastectomy with other women who have also undergone similar surgery. However, in the case, say, of people who have been receiving individual therapy to do with anxiety-based reactions and who are to join an anxiety management and support group, things are less obvious, particularly if the group leader also served as the therapist. Here it is quite likely that some, at least, will cling to the roles appropriate for individual therapy, seeking to press the group leader to focus attention on their own difficulties and, in effect, do individual therapy within the group setting. If there are members of such a group who have received no individual therapy, then it is very probable that they also will adopt the role of people coming to receive therapy. This can be very distracting and creates a pattern within a group that is sometimes referred to as 'consulting the oracle'. Because the clients have not been properly prepared, they mistake the situation as one equivalent to that of going to consult a doctor. Thus a role is adopted which is centred on the passive receipt of inquiry, examination, diagnosis, advice and procedures, a one-sided encounter in which the group leader is seen as having total responsibility and control – the opposite in fact to the way group leaders should be. When such role expectations dominate a group it will rarely achieve much of value.

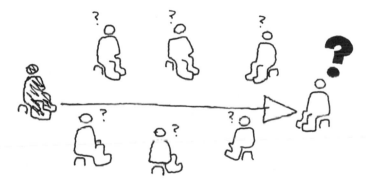

Figure 11 A one-sided encounter

Distracting emotions

The confusion caused by misconceptions and erroneous role expectations does not help either the members or the group leader and may evoke quite strong and distracting emotions. Unprepared members may be disturbed by a degree of anxiety or a defensive, angry resentment as they fail to find what they are expecting. They are likely to be taken by surprise at the type of participation needed, and the general emphasis on equal involvement and responsibility. Naturally, protest can result, sometimes in the form of a disgruntled and disruptive member urged on by others, or sometimes in the equally distracting form of a silent and withdrawn member who acts out hurt and resentment. In such circumstances the group will become sidetracked by these issues and end up way off course in relation to its real purpose.

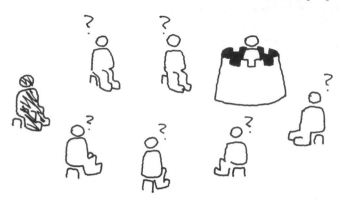

Figure 12 Silent and withdrawn

Defensive group dynamics

As mentioned in Chapter 3, one of the fascinating aspects of group behaviour is that of group psychodynamics or group process. It is not possible to give a worthwhile explanation of these complex phenomena in a few lines, although we will attempt to give a basic explanation in Chapter 6. Accept for now (if you will) that a collective or shared set of needs and associated emotions can develop in certain group circumstances, *which result in the members jointly following a particular bias in perception and expressed feelings, almost as if they were one person.* This is not usually something about which the members are overtly aware, but it shows up in the way, for example, that a shared willingness develops to talk on one issue while another issue is constantly blocked. Or again, certain conventions of behaving in relation to individuals in the group or in relation to tensions and difficult moments may be adopted as a pattern in which all the members collude. Some group theorists refer to such things as the 'collective unconscious', inferring that part of the 'engine' of group life is a shared set of unconscious processes. Be that as it may, what should be clear is that in the group naïve and wholly unprepared members may deal with the emotion generated by misconceptions and role confusion in a way which pulls in the whole group. To put it in stark terms, powerful group dynamics may develop which will wholly distort the group function and, in extreme cases, literally wreck a group.

Poor motivation, acting-out, dropping-out

The positive willingness to participate in a constructive manner forms the catalyst of a group's development. If members are ill-prepared, some will observe, deduce what the group is really about, learn, and eventually settle into being effective participants. Others will follow the opposite course. It may be a case of silent withdrawal. Occasionally, if this is not successfully dealt with by the other members and leader alike, the member may become spasmodic in attendance and then drop out of the group. It is not unknown for such an event to be accomplished with something of a flamboyant scene. Motivation is linked to hope and positive expectations. It is put at risk if a person is allowed to begin group work with little or no idea about what it entails, or worse, entirely the wrong idea. This destroys the hope, evokes a defensive cynicism and, of course, motivation fades.

Our general position on this issue must now be clear to the point of being laboured. In short, when members of a new group are required to interact in a particular way, to deal with particular kinds of issues and to achieve certain targets as a group, then it is imperative that they know about all these points and are helped in achieving them. The corollary is equally clear. The group leader must be absolutely certain in his or her own mind about the objectives and limits of the group to be run and also the types of interactions on which these depend. If the leader can specify and model the basic elements of the group, then preparation can be undertaken. If this is not possible, then effective preparation cannot be carried out. In which case, the members involved are put at some risk, as is the life of the group itself.

Effective preparation for membership in a support group

What, then, does effective preparation involve? There are at least five options available to intending leaders:

1   Preparatory *interviews* that serve as an introductory explanation and briefing.
2   Issuing carefully prepared *written notes* that convey a clear outline of the support group approach and the behaviour required for effective participation.
3   The use of an *audio recording* that gives a briefing on support groups with the inclusion of recorded extracts from a former group to illustrate what goes on in a good meeting.
4   The use of a *video recording* as a briefing on support groups illustrated by real or role-played sequences showing a support group in progress.
5   *The negotiation of a 'group contract'.* By participating in the act of

formulating a set of agreed goals and criteria to guide interaction, new group members are effectively briefed into the roles and concepts of group activity.

Inevitably, the question arises as to which approach is the best to use when starting off a support group. Much will depend on the type of people, the type of group and the objectives of the leader in setting up the group. The basic idea is that no group should ever be set up without the minimum of a carefully prepared basic briefing for intended members, followed, where possible, by a check to ensure that there are not still anxieties and confusions. The extent to which the preparations ought to be further elaborated upon is governed by the situation and resources. *Our view is that for a straightforward support group (where the function is limited to supplementing care and achieving social contact between otherwise isolated people), then a verbal explanation of the reasons for attending a group together with a short reassuring set of guidelines in written form will usually be adequate.* If resources allow these to be supplemented by pre-group contact to deal with any apprehensions or confusions which have arisen, then this makes for a fairly safe arrangement. People prone to worry about social contact may need more preparation on an individual basis.

When a support group is being formed with the possibility of undertaking more direct psychological work, for example, with depressed or anxious people, then more effort at pre-group preparation would be advisable, particularly for dealing with anxieties about the group. Similarly, when working with a group of professional people, their training may have instilled certain interactive styles and defences that are antagonistic to the type of interaction needed in a group. Thus careful pre-group preparation is called for, together with a patient modelling of required behaviour. Experience reveals, for example, that the pressure which young doctors and nurses are placed under to cope, and cover up personal stress, together with a training which encourages anxious deference towards authority figures, tends to make support groups an uncomfortable experience for many of them (Nichols 1987).

Where a more intensive approach to preparation does seem wise, then this simply means that the leader will spend more time and effort ensuring that members of a newly created group understand why they are joining a group. They need to know what type of interaction is sought, and that the group is a safe non-threatening place which offers experiences of great value. The leader will spend more time checking that the members are absorbing an accurate picture and will probably want to use more of the techniques listed above.

Almost certainly those of you who are new to group work will be concerned about the content of pre-group explanatory material. We do not, however, intend to create a set of idealized scripts for instant use. This is not evasiveness on our part but because we feel that clarifying your own ideas and intentions to a point at which you are able to express them verbally or in written form is an important formative experience. However, given that you should prepare your own material, an example is no bad thing. Below is a set of guidelines that was produced for a support group to be composed of breast cancer nurse specialists. They had asked for a support group and this was to be led by a clinical psychologist with a membership of eight nurses of mixed age and experience. The group was to meet once a month. It should be noted that these were nurses who, as part of their job, had received some basic counselling training and several of them had been in a support or training groups before – so it was not a 'beginners' group.

Notes and guidelines for the support group

Objectives – our meetings will have two objectives. First, to support one another by giving the time and effort to listen to each other's experiences in our work. We will attempt to understand what each person has encountered and what they have been feeling. Second, to help one another explore in a little greater depth the way we have approached our work and what aspects of ourselves we wish to develop or change in the job.

The group experience – the group is an experience for you to enjoy in which you can relax as your real self. At the same time it is a place to experiment with sharing personal feelings and both giving and receiving honest personal feedback.

Make the effort to 'own' feelings – in this group our attention is also directed to ourselves as a set of people relating to one another. We aim to share with each other our immediate and actual thoughts and feelings and not displace these by superficiality. Own your feelings and try to be direct, using the pronoun 'I' rather than 'we' or 'you' when you talk about feelings. The often defensive and secretive conventions of 'normal' conversation are replaced in this group by an alternative code of behaviour towards one another. We value:

- *self-discovery* – make a constant effort to pause and search out your inner feelings in relation to whatever is the focus of attention at a particular time, speak caringly but openly about this.

- *self-disclosure* – be open about your genuine feelings and thoughts and make the effort to disclose these.

Listening – make the effort to listen carefully to others in the group. Seek to discover what exactly they are experiencing rather than being preoccupied with an immediate reply or giving advice.

Support – when other members talk about personal issues and feelings, give them complete support, full attention and plenty of time.

Confronting and responding to confrontation – because of our supportive concern and involvement with one another, it can be uniquely helpful if we are direct and honest with each other. If you experience a member as avoiding an issue or failing to see something important, gently confront them with this. Those receiving such communications should pause and explore the feelings involved before rushing to reply.

The leader – the leader's role is to guide the group in the development of these ways of relating and at the same time look after the well-being of individual members. The leader is not an authority figure and will not control the group, but may at times offer suggestions to help members learn more from the experience, to help keep the group on track or to assist an individual member.

Confidentiality – our group will only succeed if we feel safe and trust each other. The specific content of the meetings and the personal details of members must be kept genuinely confidential. This is vital.

Figure 13 Giving and receiving honest personal feedback

Preparation for giving and receiving support

This book is centred around the notion of support that is provided in a group form. There is an important warning which we must make here though. It is not safe to assume that the people joining a support group will understand the nature of support. For example, *giving* support is often confused with giving advice or attempting to solve other people's problems for them. Such confusion can lead to considerable problems in the development of disruptive patterns of behaviour in a group. Similarly, not all people will know how to receive support. This is quite a familiar experience for us in running support groups for nurses (Nichols 1987), and general medical practitioners (Jenkinson and Smerdon 1988). *Receiving* support requires an understanding of what one is attempting to do in a support situation, and why anyone would do this anyway. It also requires the relaxed acceptance of certain values and attitudes. Therefore, as a final thought in this discussion on preparation, several brief guides to explaining the basic notions of support are given below. You may find it useful to present and expand on this type of material to prospective members of, say, a staff support group before beginning the group.

Receiving support – attitude and skills required

It is important to understand that seeking and receiving support is a *necessary strength* that enables de-stressing in demanding situations. Seeking support is very definitely not a sign of weakness, quite the opposite. In order to receive support, though, it is essential to be able to identify, accept and value one's own feelings and emotions and also to be able to talk openly of one's feelings and experiences with support figures. It is important to be able to trust others in support work and to receive their time, attention and care without guilt or defensiveness.

Giving support – attitude and skills required

A relaxed approach is needed and you must be able to set up a situation in which the person you are supporting feels safe and free from any form of censure or abrasive advice giving. Importantly, a person giving support has to be free of the need to solve the other person's problems personally. It also helps a lot if the support figure is free of the need to 'perform' as a therapist, that is, to solve problems and come up with insights and solutions to the other person's situation. What matters most is an ability to listen and give full and free attention. Also being at ease with the expression of feeling and the exploration of experiences by others without the need to continually intervene. Having the ability to communicate non-judgemental acceptance to the person to whom you are giving support makes the situation feel safe and enables the other to talk in more depth.

Guidelines for giving support

While a strict routine is not really appropriate when giving support, a general guide can be a useful thing to run through as a reminder just before a support session begins. The following notes cover most of the basic issues. They are set out in a form appropriate for a general work setting with colleagues supporting one another:

One to one support – guidelines

1   Make the situation feel safe – consider your style of greeting, manner, posture, and location (free from interruption or scrutiny), etc.
2   Give 'space and permission' for your colleague to talk freely at his/her own pace.
3   Initially emphasize listening, using only short guiding questions or helping statements.
4   Encourage the full expression of feeling – if this is not naturally forthcoming, gently encourage it at appropriate intervals while she/he is talking through the situation. Allow time for tears or anger when they occur – don't fuss, should there be strong feeling.
5   Emphasize showing understanding and true empathy by periodically 'reflecting back' the expressed feelings and experiences, i.e. say briefly in your own words what you have understood your colleagues to have said.
6   Avoid 'wading in' with instant advice.
7   Eventually share your own feelings and reactions – giving your reactions to what you have heard and experienced while listening. Be brief, it is your colleague's time.
8   If it is appropriate, lead her/him into thinking about and setting objectives for change or dealing with a difficult situation. Help build up a list of options but, remember, it is not your problem to solve. Conclude by helping her/him decide upon action.

5 The practicalities of starting a support group

Our review of all the issues to be considered before beginning group work is now complete. If you have come this far with us and still intend to use the group approach, then it is time to work on some practical aspects involved in actually starting up a group. As an aid we will consider a list of items about which you will have to make decisions. Some of these may seem a little basic and obvious. We make no apology for that, however, since thorough planning and preparation are necessary if professional standards are to be maintained.

Time issues for support groups

Who decides on timing?

A decision has to be reached regarding the timing, frequency, length of meetings and duration of the group. These basic features of a group often have a significant personal impact on members. For example, ease of attending is very much dictated by the timing of a group. Therefore, what might at first sight be a simple matter of administrative convenience becomes rather more complicated. This is because 'messages' matter a great deal in group work. You have to clarify who decides about the timing of your group and what message is thereby given in this arrangement. In short, are you to be a dictator, simply advertising times with which members must concur, or at the other extreme, a leader who turns the matter over to prospective members and falls in with their wishes? There is, of course, a middle ground in which the needs of all members of the group, leader included, are recognized and valued equally. Thus compromise is reached within whatever constraints circumstances dictate.

Circumstances are certainly a major determinant. A community nurse might well have to say, 'We have to start somewhere and I'm only in this part of the county on Monday afternoons or Thursday mornings so it will have to be an hour during one of those two time slots.' This represents the 'bottom line' beyond which the nurse cannot budge. Beyond that perhaps there would be room for manoeuvre.

It is important to establish a structure within which people feel safe and free in talking about their needs. Clear and effective modelling is therefore very important in helping people register that they are safe and free. The process should begin by using this opportunity to encourage members in declaring their needs regarding timing. This allows you to arrange things so that the members can experience their needs as being recognized and valued, even though compromise solutions might have to be worked out.

Quite commonly leaders declare a time for an initial meeting and then negotiate the whole matter of times with the rest of the members at that initial meeting. If this approach suits you, state your 'bottom line' limits in a businesslike, neutral way, and help the group with the negotiations. Incidentally much may be learned of the likely functioning within your group while this goes on. It can serve as a 'try your strength event' with members aware of who exerts pressure to get their own way and how the leader handles it.

Occasionally there will be an impasse. If there is no obvious solution a decision will have to be taken by the leader to resolve it. If the arrangement excludes one or two people, then consider some other form of support for them, or inclusion in a later group. A good policy is to inform potential members of the likely time bands from which a regular meeting time will have to be chosen. This can be done with the offer of membership in the group.

Frequency of meetings

As with so much in group work, there is no accepted correct practice regarding frequency. A good place to start is by considering a weekly meeting. More than this, and the group can assume a very high profile in the life of the members, with high carry-over from one group to the next. The risk here is that the group can itself become a way of life rather than a means to a better one. Even at once a week, the group is likely to figure prominently for the members. In between meetings they are very likely to go on re-living exchanges from the group and will continue to think about and digest them. Quite often they will arrive at the next meeting ready to carry on the theme of the last meeting.

If the interval between meetings is increased, this effect becomes less noticeable, so that groups meeting every four weeks or longer often need to spend time re-grouping, updating, remembering and reminding before settling down to work. The longer interval does give time for reflection and time to develop a sense of proportion about things said in the group. There will also have been time to put into practice things learnt in the group, if need be, to try things out and see if they work. Much will depend on the members' needs and situation. If, say, you are beginning a support group for some caregivers of people with Alzheimer's disease, it could well be that once a month is all that the members can manage without the group becoming another burden in life. Once a week for a palliative care nurses' support group could be seen as an ideal to aim for but it would almost certainly prove impractical and destined to become another demand on the nurses' busy schedules. In these two cases a monthly meeting is more realistic.

How long should support group meetings be?

Encounters of almost any duration can have their value, but a good working average seems to be about one to one-and-a-half hours. This span gives time for meeting, greeting, settling down, work, summing-up, closure and good-byes, with time available somewhere in the middle if people have something they really need to work on. Less time than this, and something is likely to suffer. A feeling of being under time pressure can get in the way and affect the group adversely. The span needs to be long enough for members to feel it was 'worth coming'. At the same time, excessive length which goes beyond the members' or leader's attention span is clearly unwise.

Note in passing that if, in later meetings, the time seems to be going more slowly than usual, and your attention keeps straying, it might be a good idea to find a way of sharing this with the group. After all, if it's simply that you are tired, they would find it helpful to know this. But it may be that they are feeling the same way too, and if that is so, there are at least two possibilities. The first is that there is something structurally wrong – the room is too hot, airless, or the timing is wrong and the group is being held when people are tired from work. But the second, and more likely reason is that there is some sort of message around for deciphering. It could be for instance that the group was avoiding something serious, using their tiredness to avoid doing the work, or simply waiting for the leader to 'tell them off' and urge them to get back to the work that the group is there for. Either way it can be useful to explore it together.

There are some types of group whose meetings go on for much longer than one and a half hours, some as long as several days, but they are beyond the scope of this volume. It is not recommended that those of you beginning as group leaders should try your hand at extended groups until you have greatly widened your experience. (For a further discussion, see Yalom 1985.)

What 'start-up' format and timing should support groups have?

Throughout the group's entire life it is likely that you, as leader, will have a powerful influence on format, that is the handling of events within the group. Early on, the members will probably look to you to tell them what to do, when to do it, in what order, and for how long. As discussed earlier, it is within the leader's power to give away some of the tasks and see to it that the group takes on some responsibility for the pattern and timing of the work to be done. She or he can make it clear that she or he is not prepared to carry sole responsibility, and request that everyone helps decide how things are to be done. However, this may be asking too much of a new group and a new leader right at the start before both have settled down and found their feet. If you are in this situation, it might be worthwhile asking if the group has got views on the way to arrange meetings as far as the timing and length are concerned.

In our view, it is part of the initial duty of the leader to ensure that the group becomes time-conscious and develops an awareness of how much time is available to do what. It is not unusual for groups to find it hard to start, so that it is important to establish whether a timing of '3.00–4.30' means 'arrive at 3.00 for coffee, toilets, coat-hanging, biscuits, and hellos, for a 3.20 start, and finish at 4.50', or what? Members may be justifiably cross if they have moved heaven and earth to arrive punctually only to find the group doesn't really start for another 20 minutes. A clear agreement should be made.

In matters of punctuality, it is as well for the leader at least to stick to agreed times, and be ready to start on time, no matter how the members might conduct themselves. Some attention needs to be paid to the issue of 'better late than never' so that everyone knows what the ground rules are if they are forced to decide whether, if they are delayed, to arrive late or miss the meeting. A clear ground rule so that everyone knows the group preference and is prepared to take responsibility for their own behaviour and time-keeping helps.

However long it takes to settle down, there will come a point at which everyone is (at last) ready, and the leader has to be alert for that moment. It will usually be marked non-verbally, by most or all eyes being upon the leader, and a stillness, perhaps a brief moment of total quiet. If it's missed, the leader may find it quite difficult to bring everyone back to the same point of readiness again.

How many meetings, and over what period of time?

Again, there are no firm guidelines, but a great deal of opinion. Perhaps the important thing is to make sure the issue is properly addressed and resolved at the beginning, or in preparatory sessions. There is a difference in kind between short-term, medium-term and long-term groups (the last may actually aim to be semi-permanent). Much depends on the aims of the support group and whether it is of fixed or open membership. Some people can benefit enormously from just one meeting, others need much more. Ongoing support groups may be permanent but with a changing membership. It is for you to make a balanced judgement on this issue. However, do not forget to ask yourself how long you wish the commitment to run for. A device which we have both used is that of running for a fixed term, say, ten meetings and then deciding, as a group, whether to run for another ten.

Venues for support groups

Support groups can be held in a variety of places. We have both had to contend with some pretty unfavourable conditions on occasions but this obviously is not recommended. One group recently had to manage with a flimsy portable display screen as the only physical barrier between their space and a busy, noisy corridor, but it did not appear to hinder group business too much. However, it is obvious that you need to have as much going in your favour as possible.

Perhaps the most important thing is to have a space over which you have some authority. For example, a prestigious group leader had been persuaded by a friend to conduct a group for volunteer helpers. A room was duly booked at the local college, and all was going well until the door was thrown open by the caretaker, who jangled a big bunch of keys and demanded that whatever it was that was being done should stop as he personally had not been informed and wanted to go home. Assertiveness of the highest order was called for that disrupted the atmosphere of the group.

This story demonstrates the importance of uninterruptability, of being able to post a sign saying 'Do not disturb' with some confidence that it will be respected. Hazards to be avoided, if possible, are other users of the building walking in to ask directions, the telephone, and according to the time of day, cleaning staff, or one's own superiors who may feel they have right of access, uninvited and unannounced. At the same time, the room does need to be easily accessible, somewhere central for members to get to without undue difficulty. Amenities of great interest are adequate refreshment and toilet facilities – somewhere to make a cup of coffee can be of more than cosmetic use to the group, a way of having a breather if need be.

Finally, some thought should be given to the furnishing, decoration and lighting of the room (if there is the luxury of a choice of rooms that is). It is a good plan to have enough comfortable chairs for everyone, and if they are all similar in style, so much the better. Swinging and rocking chairs should be avoided, as should the provision of 'special' chairs for the leader. Some people are uncomfortable with the harsh glare of fluorescent lights.

Most leaders work with the chairs in an approximate circle, with no other furniture on the inside of the group, and no undue spaces or empty chairs between the members. Early on, the group can find itself worrying about the empty chair of a latecomer/possible absentee, and wondering at length whether to remove the chair and complete the circle, against the awkwardness if the absentee should arrive and there be no place for them. As with many other issues, the leader is wise to let the group settle it, develop their own way of handling things. He or she could, for instance, simply say 'What do we do about the empty chair?' and wait.

Membership of support groups

The initial decisions concerning membership will normally fall to the group leader. It is an important issue with various considerations.

Size of the group

For practical purposes a good size for a support group is somewhere between six and ten members. Below this, the group can lose its dynamism, and become much more akin to an observed personal counselling session, which may not be quite what the members had in mind. In so small a group it is not unusual for people to feel unduly exposed, with nowhere they can hide if they feel like it.

With more than ten members, it becomes increasingly difficult to keep track of the flow of events, the formation of sub-groups, and to ensure 'fair shares for all'. The energies running in bigger groups are often harder to cope with. People have to speak louder in more ways than one to make themselves heard. Some may be overawed, and say nothing, when they would be able to manage in a smaller group.

Composition

The selection of people to make up the membership of a support group must be done with thought and caution. When considering people as possible members, ask yourself, 'Is this person likely to benefit from the group and will he or she contribute to it (perhaps eventually), without being too disruptive meanwhile?' Useful characteristics to look out for in would-be members are:

- Some willingness to listen to, consider, and have respect for other people's experience.
- Not to have so great a need that they are likely to dominate the group to the exclusion of others.
- To be able to fit in with the general profile of other group members and group objectives. For example, being able to explore experiences rather than intruding with instant advice.
- Acceptance of the stated aims and methods of the group.
- Trustworthiness with reference to respecting the confidences of others.

We have mentioned before the desirability of having the concerns of the support group contained within reasonable boundaries. In our earlier example of the pain group, it would have been inappropriate to have included someone with quite different concerns to the other group members, for instance, someone with addiction or relationship problems. A wide range of concerns within the group may be manageable by highly skilled therapists, but we think should be avoided by inexperienced leaders. Similarly, avoid including people who suffer obvious major psychological or behavioural problems within a simple support group. Their presence may distort the group functioning and hamper progress towards objectives. This is not to say that such people do not merit care or would not benefit from a group approach, but rather that untrained people should not attempt to run therapy groups, which is what would be needed in such cases. Thus, when considering your group: people needing support – yes; people needing therapy – no (unless you have training).

Open versus closed membership for support groups

In other words, should the membership be fixed for the life of the group or is there to be a continual coming and going of members with the passing of time? Circumstances may well dictate on this, as in some of the examples given in Chapter 2. A long-running support group may have changed its membership almost entirely within a year in one setting (e.g. a coronary rehabilitation support group) whereas a staff group might be stable for a year or more. Thus, once your initial group has settled down, it may well be that it soon has to face the question of whether to close its doors to new members, or negotiate the conditions under which they may be admitted. There is no right or wrong way – it will depend on the type of group and the situation involved. Quite often the situation is dealt with by having support groups of a fixed membership but with a limited life of six to ten meetings after which a new group is started.

If the group is to be closed to new members, there will need to be a clear statement from the leader that below a certain attendance figure the group is no longer viable. Clear advantages of the closed group are that it develops a history of its own and does not have to pause to explain things to newcomers. Nor does it have the risk of being impeded by 'group naïve' newcomers or have to wait for them to catch up.

If the support group is open, it will need to be agreed just what is the basis for admission. Does the intending newcomer have to be approved by all the group, or just the leader? It would be wise to discuss such matters thoroughly before strangers are admitted. In any event, the leader will need to be on the alert until any newcomers are integrated into the group, a process that can involve some kind of testing of the new arrival by older members. Such testing is likely to be largely unconscious, but nevertheless real, and some caution will be present in the group until they feel they have the measure of

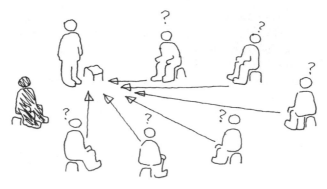

Figure 14 Testing the new arrival

the newcomer, and once again become a group. In a nutshell, the introduction of new members to any existing group should be done with care.

The what, how and when of the first session

You have now reached the point where your chosen members are arriving for their first group session. It may also be your first experience of being a leader, in which case be reassured that a little nervousness is not unusual.

Managing the first few minutes of the first session

The leader needs to be helpful in settling everyone down. With novice, hesitant or unsure members a reassuring presence reminiscent of the good host or hostess allows a tension-free beginning. Because of your previous experience or preparation for the start-up of your group, you ought to be on 'home territory' or, at least, more so than the members and so will be well placed to see to it that people are greeted and made at ease. We are not suggesting that this should be overdone, people do not need smothering or fussing over but rather, there is a good opportunity to help people feel a bit more relaxed. There are certain types of personal growth groups where making people feel relaxed is not the intention of the leaders, the belief being that confusion and ambivalence provide profitable ground to explore. However, in the straightforward support group it is pointless and unkind to allow people to flounder needlessly. What is more, an absence of effort on the part of the leader to put members at ease may actually create agitation in the group, giving the leader a harder job to get the group moving.

Thus, you should be working towards several objectives. First, to greet members and settle them into the circle. Second, to introduce members or, in a larger group, arrange some way for names to be made known and learnt. We find it useful to give everyone a 6-inch strip of card on which they print their name. This is then displayed on the floor against their chair for the first couple of meetings. If preferred, pin-on name badges are readily available. Third, to check that everybody understands and agrees to the objectives of the group and its way of running. This may prove more complicated than you expect – so go through the following carefully to prepare yourself.

We cannot cover all contingencies but will assume that you are running either a client or staff support group. We further assume that you will have had some face-to-face contact with the members and gone through some of the preparatory work outlined in Chapter 3. Thus members will either already be well acquainted with the 'contract' (although not perhaps with this term being used) or will at least have received some written material from you.

Despite this, with an entirely new group, be prepared for the discussion of purpose and ground rules to extend into the first session. For the future positive development of the group it will be preferable for the members knowingly to opt into the group. To do this sensibly they will need to have a clear idea of the purpose of the group, some idea of the leader's style, that is, how he or she proposes to behave, and a notion of what behaviour by the members will be seen as appropriate, acceptable and productive. These can therefore be important discussions which set the code of conduct for the next few meetings. It may come as a disappointment that, despite earlier discussion or having distributed an outline of the group contract, some members do not understand it. It happens. For example at the first meeting of a nurses' support group, a nurse manager arrived and opened a notebook ready to make notes, an action which betrayed a complete misunderstanding of what the group was about. Similarly at a coronary unit's multidisciplinary support group, an ill-informed consultant arrived late and then asked for a copy of the agenda from 'madam chairperson'. Such gross disorientation has to be dealt with by a review of the contract which you have devised, so have some copies handy. In the latter example the leader eventually gave a second verbal briefing to the group on its purpose and nature. This briefing by the leader went as follows:

> This is to be a staff support group, in other words, it should help us to manage the more difficult parts of our jobs and, hopefully, help to keep stress levels down. If it is to work, we have to make the group feel a safe place, a place where we can talk freely and reveal our experiences and feelings without any need to be on our guard. This is so important that I hope we can use the guidelines that group leaders normally adopt. In which case our aim will be to do the following:
>
> • Enable each other to talk about anything that is currently important to us concerning our work, relationships or experiences in this group.

- Make sure that each member is listened to carefully and that their experiences are properly understood and explored.
- Help each other express feelings more deeply and honestly rather than giving instant advice or opinion.
- Avoid irrelevant or trivial diversions (check with the group if you are not sure).
- Avoid generalities and make your ownership of personal feelings clear, thus saying, 'I feel' rather than 'you or one feels'.
- Guarantee confidentiality and also avoid the discussion of group issues outside the group – thus taking away some of its life.

The leader's role is to try to help the group achieve these ideals.

In presenting such a statement, the leader is also making a statement about how he or she sees her role. The leader has taken the initiative, a first and strong move to establish the framework within which the group will run. A basis for negotiation has been laid down and appropriate behaviours described. The statement makes it clear that the leader intends to be helpful, a facilitator who gets things going, without being a commanding officer in charge of everything. Crucially, the issue of confidentiality has been broached.

Hopefully, none of this will come as a surprise, as potential members should have been introduced to the list beforehand, and given a chance to think about it. Nevertheless, there may still be an early period of bargaining and clarifying where people will wish to question and perhaps put their own stamp on the 'contract'. It is sometimes hard to say whether this energetic business is part of the group sequence proper, or simply a necessary preliminary settling-in, a 'getting things straight' introduction. It is much more likely in a multidisciplinary staff support group than in a client support group, where the leader is less likely to be challenged. One of the author's recent experiences with the whole staff of a medical unit (medical nursing, technical, etc.) has served as a useful reminder that negotiations concerning the purpose and manner of operation of a staff group can become long and fraught. The major part of the first three meetings were dominated with the theme of 'the purpose of the group'.

Thus, one group may easily settle into its stride with no problems, while another will fall to protracted argument over the details. In this latter case, the alert leader will think about whether the amount of uproar being generated is out of all proportion to the significance of the issue, and will look to see what's behind it all, where all the fuel is coming from. It is tempting, but unrewarding, to pin labels on such behaviour, and think to oneself, 'They're being really childish, why are they making such a fuss?' or 'Why on earth are they pretending not to understand, as if the words are really difficult?' Care and patience are called for. However, anticipating the next chapter, the most likely explanation is that group process is behind it all, that is, a collective, unspoken feeling is guiding the behaviour of the members.

Be that as it may, everyone will be bringing to their first group meeting a bundle of hopes, anxieties, ideas and feelings that are likely to find expression one way or another in the group business. Some new members are likely to be feeling nervous and apprehensive to some degree. This can mean that they fall silent or, alternatively, find themselves saying things more vigorously than they normally would. The gentle, relaxed presence of the support group leader will usually help ease away such difficulties.

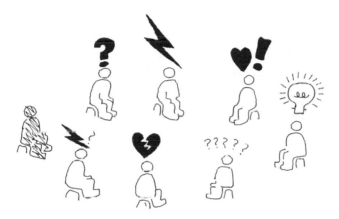

Figure 15 A bundle of hopes, anxieties, ideas and feelings

Setting going 'group business'

There will come a time when the settling-in and agreeing terms are over. What exactly does the leader say to set things going? All that is needed is a simple invitation which acts as a signal for a change of mood and entry into the group session. For example, one of the following phrases may be used to lead a group into its real work, both during the first session and in later meetings:

- We must begin. Since this is our first meeting and none of you know one another, it will be helpful if each member introduces him or herself and gives a very brief background covering the last few months.
- I think that it is time we started. We might begin by saying a little about our background and how we feel at this moment.
- OK, if everybody is settled, we can get going. Check with yourself how you are feeling and what experiences you have gone through recently and then see if you would like to share these with the group.

It is not suggested that you should learn such lines parrot-fashion, and churn them out. The idea is to present you with some alternatives (to which we hope you will add your own) that you may choose from. Imagine yourself starting the group, think of what you want to say, and of your own way of saying it, so that you won't feel pressured by being caught out and flustered. When it comes to the actual opening, it is as well just to relax and say something simple and natural to start things off. Knowing that you have thought out a way of starting should help you to relax because you know you always have something to fall back on. If you feel stuck, select one of our lines above nearest in meaning to what you want to say, and use that. Say it, then wait.

In making your selection, we would like you to keep in mind your short-term aims and objectives for this first meeting. A good way of clarifying what these might be is to ask yourself what you are hoping for by the end of the meeting. What do you hope will have happened? It is useful to think in both general and more specific terms. 'Aims' consist of more generalized ambitions, such as 'to have got the group settled down and beginning to work'. 'Objectives' are more specific behavioural goals, countable in a 'yes or no' sort of way. An example would be 'everyone should have spoken at least once by the end of the first meeting'.

Right now would be a good time to pause and ask yourself just what it is you have in mind for your intended group, if you haven't done so already, and actually write down a few first lines of your own. Just what are you going to try and do, and how you will know when you have done it? Is this possible to ascertain?

You may find it useful to eavesdrop on an interview with Jacquie, a community worker who has decided to run a group for the elderly. Most of her clients are finding it hard to do as much as they once did, feeling their aches and pains, and grumbling a bit. Some are on their own following be-reavement, are lonely, but ambivalent at coming to any 'old folks' functions, not least the group. What is Jacquie looking for by the end of her first meeting?

J.:   Well, I suppose the most important thing is that they will have settled down a bit, feel less awkward, and got over their first nervousness at talking about themselves to strangers. I would like them to feel a bit more at home, that this is somewhere they belong, that they will like coming to and get something positive from the meetings.

Interviewer: That sounds reasonable enough. How will you manage it?

J.:   I will make sure at the start that I feel OK about things and won't be put off if they are a bit difficult or uncooperative at first. After all, they won't really know what to say, and if they are nervous they won't be at their best. So I will try and make sure everyone gets spoken to by somebody right at the beginning, just before we start properly. If someone looks as if they are feeling specially awkward or left out, I will talk to them myself, you know, just conversation about getting here, the weather, anything.

Interviewer: You don't think they should be just left to get on with it?

J.: No. Everybody likes to be made to feel welcome when they go somewhere new, and the group is no exception. As I am the one who knows most about what is happening, what we are doing, I think it is up to me to ease things along at the beginning, if I can. It helps too if I can find a way to let people know they are not freakish for feeling nervous or uncertain. I can say that while no-one can be sure exactly what is going to happen, I am confident that the group will be able to come together and get some benefit by sharing experiences, feelings and ideas. I will explain that I don't have all the answers, so it is no good expecting me to, but that the group has within it what answers there are, we just have to find them.

Interviewer: That all sounds a bit vague. Won't saying that just worry people more?

J.: Mmm, yes, you may be right. But I will have to find some way in the first session of letting them know I am not the oracle to be consulted for the answer to all difficulties – we have all got a hand in whether the group comes together or not, so it is no good sitting back and expecting me to work the miracle. I suppose that is a bit severe, but it has got to be established that everyone is responsible for the group's well-being, not just the leader. I had better not say all that straight off, as it is important to get them talking early on, but I will be looking for the chance to say it before the end of the first session. I will be very careful what I say as I know that at first they are likely to pay exaggerated attention to me, and can be very sensitive.

Interviewer: You say it is important they should talk early on. How will you manage that?

J.: I will say straight off that I do not intend to do all the talking, and then ask an 'open' question, one that invites their contribution, such as 'How is everybody feeling today?' Then I will wait and see what happens. It will feel like forever, but it will probably only be a second or two before somebody speaks. If the wait should go on for more than, say, half a minute, I'll say something like, 'We seem to be finding it hard to start. Any ideas as to why that might be, what is in the way?' And if that does not work, finally I will suggest a way forward, like saying our names, or something about ourselves, or saying hello to our immediate neighbours in the group, tell them why you have come, then try again. But really I expect that within a few seconds somebody will have started us off. Probably they will suggest introductions of some sort, then everybody gets a chance to say something and get over their nerves.

Interviewer: Is there anything else you will be hoping for by the end of the first session?

J.:   Yes. I would like them to have a clearer idea of what the group is like, how it will run, what use it might be. I would like them to leave feeling good, interested and looking forward to coming next time, perhaps pleasantly surprised that it was not as bad as they thought it was going to be. Also I would like them to have experienced some feeling of companionship, a sense of not being quite so alone in facing their lives. It should not have been an ordeal.

Interviewer: Will you be able to tell whether you have been successful?

J.:   Probably. I will get a good idea from listening carefully to the tenor of what is being said, especially in the more off-guard moments like breaking off for a cup of tea, or putting on coats to go home. Even more important, perhaps, I will be watching really carefully, because it is not unusual for people to be polite in what they say, but their behaviour, their bodies, are saying something different. There may be a tightness around the mouth, a frown, a stiffness about the shoulders, a reluctance to talk to others, anything. And, of course, there is an acid test in whether they come back.

Interviewer: You have told me where you hope the members will have got to. How about yourself, what do you hope for yourself?

J: I think for myself I would like to think that I have managed to stay centred, not to have been thrown off course by anything that has happened in the group. I want to have managed to be an example of constructive group behaviour, offering a model for the members to observe and think about. Some of the things in our working group contract sound deceptively easy, but in practice can be difficult. For instance, really listening to another person without one's own thoughts, feelings, judgements, opinions and good advice intruding is actually quite hard. It is useful to see it being done, or to experience it for oneself. In everyday life it's so tempting to offer 'helpful advice', to pretend to 'know best', but in the group you need to think twice before doing that. By the end of the session I hope that everyone accepts that they have some responsibility to make the group work, and not just leave it up to me to run everything. I want to be treated well by the group, not adored, not ignored, not attacked, not put down, and certainly not treated as a guru, or some authority figure to be appeased or battled with.

It is clear that overall Jacquie has a good feel for where she wants the group to get to, and has it in mind to look for specific objectives for herself and for the members.

To recapitulate: we had got as far as considering the first possible statements that a leader might make when starting the first meeting of a support group. This led us into a survey of the need for clear aims and objectives. In Jacquie's interview she outlines how she sees herself continuing after her opening statement. Perhaps her most significant phrases are 'I do not want to do all the talking' ... 'Then, I will wait'. We would expect that after the invitation to begin there might well be a short silence. Do not panic about this, usually it is not that long a silence. As a new leader, it is all too easy to believe that it is down to you to rescue the situation immediately, that it is your fault if things are not going smoothly instantly. It is as well not to rush in too quickly, though. Allow your group time to find its feet and begin conversation. Relax with the silence. Intervene only if the group cannot seem to make a start or if, after a while, it seems to be going down the wrong path.

The first hour of the first meeting

The practicalities have been dealt with. The contract or group briefing has been dealt with too. It is the moment to begin and this has been signalled with your chosen opening phrases. What happens now and how critical is your performance as leader in determining whether or not the group succeeds in its first meeting?

It is inappropriate to say that at this point the work of the leader is done and that he or she should now relax and let it all unfold. There is, however, a sense in which something like this might apply for a period, depending on the type of group and the atmosphere which develops. Sometimes leaders are called group facilitators. This catches the idea that we cannot control a group as if the members were a set of puppets. We can only do so much – set up the meetings, compose the group, settle the members in with instructions on the objectives of the group and the appropriate ways of relating during the meetings, model appropriate self-disclosure and make supporting comments directed to those members who take up the task of participating. However, we cannot compel the members to interact in the fashion that we want. Thus, to a degree, the leader does have to go 'hands off' and give the group freedom to develop. Excessive over-protective or fussy intervention simply sets the group back. Having said that, some interventions on your part may be very helpful. Gently inviting members to continue to introduce themselves if the conversation becomes sidetracked. Assisting members who seem rather tongue-tied or overawed by the situation. Making space for less assertive members if one or two of the group are rather dominant and 'occupy' a disproportionate amount of the conversation time in the meeting.

There is also always the possibility in a support group that includes members who have had distressing or traumatizing experiences that, despite a light-hearted and relatively superficial beginning, emotion will begin to surface and one or more of those present will become tearful or emotional in some other way. Part of the reason for them being in the group is to have the opportunity to express feeling and so this is a normal part of support group life – although it might feel a little premature if members have barely learned each other's names. Try to deal with 'emotional moments' in a natural relaxed way. Above all, do not become tense and awkward with the situation. Little bits of guidance can help the group and also an increase in physical support and contact greatly eases the tension of emotional expression away. For example, Pat became tearful while talking about her feelings after her premature child died and, in another group, Don choked to a silence trying not to be tearful when talking at a care-givers' support group about the impact on him of his wife's stroke:

> Cheryl – can you move a little closer to Pat and put your arm round her for a little physical support while she talks to us about her experiences?

and

> Dave – there's no need to fight back emotion, everybody here has gone through and felt something similar. If we make our circle a little tighter around you and if Wendy just links her arm with you, maybe you can say a bit more to us about how it all happened.

Obviously the first meeting of a support group can go in many different directions and there is no way in which we can tackle all of these here. However, we will consider two types of 'first meeting atmosphere' that can occur and comment on how you, as leader, might deal with them.

The enthusiastic client/patient support group

Many support groups are of the type that we have described in the preceding chapters. The members will be clients or patients who are suffering some form of disability or distress, or alternatively the group will be composed of their partners. After some minutes of finding things a little strange and thus feeling awkward, groups like this will often burst into excited life. The relief of being with fellow sufferers who truly understand, and of being able to speak freely, opens the flood gates. A warm sense of cohesion grows together with a shared sense of relief. You, as leader, will probably need to do little at this juncture, although this may change in later meetings. Monitor what patterns emerge, who dominates and who retreats, how the members respond to one another and what use they make of you. Beyond this, the session is about meeting and relaxing into support. Thus, you can just let it unfold for much of the session. The occasional guiding remark will keep a general sense of direction, for example, 'Most of you have spoken about your general situation and what has been happening lately but Tim and Jill are still a bit of a mystery. Maybe they would like to tell us how things are for them, otherwise we will run out of time before they have a chance.'

The strained staff support group

Despite the best of intentions the first meeting of a support group can, on occasions, be painful and disappointing. The members can seem very hesitant and tense. The atmosphere will be troubled by confusion and floundering with the more threatened members making the running with irrelevancies. Awkward silences can raise the tension. If this happens, it is possibly because the preparation has been inadequate or because the membership is unbalanced in some way. For example, an oncology clinical nurse manager asked for a support group for her nurses. No preparation was possible except at the occasion of the first meeting and no selection for membership was possible since all the staff were to attend, that is trainees, staff nurses, two sisters and the nurse manager. The younger nurses who had originally suggested the need for a support group to the clinical nurse manager later revealed that, in the event, they felt intimidated. They worried that if they were truly open about the difficulties they felt at times they would be judged badly by what they said and that this might be put on their records. Needless to say, these nurses froze and the group became the opposite of a warm and supportive environment. In fact, this particular group never did recover and it foundered after three sessions. A classic example of how not to do it.

Hopefully, you will not have to deal with this sort of atmosphere but if you are starting off a staff support group, be prepared for a slow start. The warm rush of sharing that was described in the client group may not develop. There may instead be a progressive increase in trust and depth as the weeks go by. If the first meeting is a little slow and awkward, again you must accept this and not get too embroiled in dragging the group wherever you want them to go. They may need lots of time for testing things out, finding their way and developing trust. It is a time for you to remain free of panic and hold back thoughts like 'It's all my fault, I'm no good as a leader'. Model appropriate group behaviour by sharing your concern that the group feels a little insecure and that things are not going as well as you had hoped. Groups are about sharing issues, including the leader's concern for the group. Gently remind the group of what the objectives are and try to lead them back from irrelevant pastimes or defensive ploys, e.g. 'We seem to have fallen into discussing cases. This group is really intended as a place for us to discuss our world, not that of the patients. Perhaps we can get back to that by reviewing our last few days and how we have felt during that time.'

Ending the first meeting

We regard finishing on time as a fairly important discipline to be observed. Paradoxically, once over any initial reticence at speaking it is not unusual for groups to pick up such momentum that they lose sight of time going by. The good leader will have taken care to establish the finishing time, and should make sure that he or she has easy access to the time, preferably without continually glancing at the clock. Similarly, the good leader needs to develop a feeling for how much time there remains, for he or she has some responsibility to gear the work being done to the time available. The experience of being really listened to, possibly for the first time ever, can be very powerful for people in a group. Members may find themselves deeply moved by the support and companionship that can be present, even in a first meeting, and as a consequence open up personal areas usually kept well hidden. Until the group has learnt the importance of ending on time, and monitoring their own work accordingly, you, as leader, will have to do it for them. It would be most unfair not to bring to the group's attention that there was insufficient time left to do justice to any further deep material that might emerge. Members who have already moved into very personal areas and may even, to their amazement, have cried a little during the group will now need time to compose themselves and settle down for the group's end and the journey home. As the meetings go by, both you and your group will develop a feel for what is manageable in the time left. As a 'rule of thumb', you should look for an opportunity towards the end of the group to remind everyone that there is only a little time left, usually somewhere between 15 and 5 minutes remaining. Less than 5 minutes hardly gives anyone a chance to finish any remaining business. Say something like, 'I think we need to draw things to a close now', and let the group look after tidying up. Towards the very end, a good question to put to the group is 'Does anyone still have anything left they want to say to anyone?'

6 Underway
The middle stages of a
support group

You will probably have gathered by now that the strategy which we have used to help us present our material is to visualize ourselves talking to you as if you were actually engaged in starting up a support group and we were to be your consultant-supervisors. Thus, we have now arrived at the stage where you are established as the leader of a support group that has begun to meet at regular intervals. The next task is to consider the important issues and concerns as the group develops and approaches maturity.

Whitaker (1985) views the groups that she leads as moving through three phases. The first of these is the *formative phase*. It may last for part of all of the first meeting and can, in some groups, go well beyond this into subsequent meetings. During the formative phase the members struggle with the task of establishing themselves as a group which feels like it will last and in which they feel they have a place. The key elements to getting established are a sense of safety and structure (by which is meant the expected behaviour, activities and roles which are required in the group). During the formative phase there is usually a degree of uncertainty and hesitation until members know and trust one another and safety and structure are established. In the type of support group that we are considering the leader must bear such needs in mind. The members will need time to be together and build up knowledge and awareness of each other. Attempts at working towards the objectives of the group contract may be in the form of rather brief episodes of 'testing the water' followed by a retreat into something which feels more like everyday conversation. In this phase the leader needs to adopt a gentle, patient style always ready to help with the task on hand. This means taking a hand in helping the members getting to know each other. Thus it is possible to build up a rapport, gently coaching the members into what is appropriate and not appropriate in the group. We can try allowing 'defensive respite' when the group seems threatened by attempts at work, and then leading them back to take a look at the situation to develop safe ways of handling it. Examples of such action are given in the next section.

The formative phase of a group gives way to the so-called *established phase*. The concerns of the formative phase start to fade, the group is experienced by the members as viable, safe and worthwhile. It has 'gelled' and accordingly becomes less defensive, more open and more able to deal with the personal and feeling-based issues that are the basis of support work. The group has, effectively, matured. The third phase has to do with a group drawing to a close and is, naturally enough, termed the *termination phase*. It concerns letting go, anxiety, and grieving. Chapter 7 deals with this at length while the rest of this chapter is about leading a group in its established phase.

In general, Whitaker's outline of phases seems sensible and familiar. It serves as a very general guide to changes of atmosphere that can be expected in your group. The only point to emphasize is that if a group which appears to have passed through its formative phase and settled down undergoes an alarming experience which disturbs the fabric of safety, the group may temporarily revert to a guarded, cautious atmosphere reminiscent of the early meetings. Similarly the departure, or possibly the death of a member, may bring about a temporary atmosphere akin to the termination phase.

'Yes, but what do you actually do?' *facilitating* versus leading

Exact procedures can be very comforting. They give a sense of direction and freedom from the worry of needing to make decisions or take initiatives in an ambiguous situation. Groups are decidedly ambiguous situations at times and, since inexperienced leaders are usually insecure, you may well be hopeful now that we are about to give an exact set of procedures for running your group. We do not know of any group leaders (including the authors) who have not anxiously asked, 'What exactly should I do?' *The straight truth is that there are no exact procedures. The anxieties of leadership have to be dealt with in other ways.*

Perhaps the most important insight that you need in relation to this problem is that, although we have used the term 'leader', in reality, the role which you will play in your support group is more that of a 'facilitator'. Of course, there are certain basic leadership responsibilities that we will shortly describe in full. However, unlike, say, a seminar, for which you would have to construct an agenda and then organize the meeting in a planned way in order to make sure that certain ground is covered, facilitating a group is far less directive. *The notion is more to do with assisting the group rather than leading it.* Therefore, one assists the group in clarifying its objectives and points out whenever the group appears to have lost sight of these. Similarly, one assists the group in establishing a theme to explore, or helps in negotiations as to who will present material, how much time is to be set aside for this and how reactions to it will be voiced. As we show in the following sections, the leader also helps by being the 'guarantor' of safety in the group and by intervening to aid understanding and learning, with comments on patterns and processes in the group. This last form of contribution is something that depends on experience in groups and is not something that a new leader will necessarily want to attempt early on. Later, with experience, reading, and discussion with someone in a supervising role, initial attempts at facilitating by commenting on group patterns can begin.

In understanding the notion of facilitating a group, one of the most vital realizations is that, for the average member of a group, *the process is often as important as specific content.* By this we mean that the act of belonging to a group and experiencing its atmosphere and activity is as important as the specific ground covered and specific things said. Thus, your interventions as leader should not be approached with apprehension and 'performance' nerves, under normal circumstances they are not that critical in this type of group. Similarly, and within reason, the kind of presence you maintain as a leader, the interpersonal style that you model, the general stance you take towards the members and the things that they say, and your relaxed openness to the expression of feelings, are as important in a support group as specific pronouncements on your part. That is, *how you are with the group may be actually more important than what you say.* Certainly, there are going to be occasions when, for example, an intervention by a leader draws a group back from defensive, time-wasting irrelevance. Likewise, as we illustrated in the preceding chapter, in the early meetings of a wholly inexperienced set of members, helpful, guiding remarks and suggestions by the leader will act as a 'route plan' for the members and will lead to a more rapid development of cohesion and sense of purpose. A mature support group is not so dependent on the leader, in fact, some will function adequately if the leader is ill and misses a meeting. Thus, it is your long-term influence and presence that form the real issues in your performance as a group leader, rather than smart comments or penetrating analysis at any one time.

Maybe this sounds daunting and evokes an even stronger plea of 'Yes, but what do I actually have to do?' We have to stress that much of the activity of the leader will be responding to what is happening and it is in this sense that we say that there can be few set procedures. *The leader has to set the group running and react to whatever comes up. He or she cannot impose a set of activities on a support group since these would have more to do with the leader's needs than those of the group and would stultify the natural development within a group.* Similarly, since each group is unique, it is useless to attempt to formulate exact responses to situations. These have to be judged at the time. However, we can and will give some general guidelines on things to look out for and a general approach by which to run your group.

Initially, it may be helpful to take brief snapshots from moments in the history of a particular group and to link these to the leader's thoughts and interventions at the time. This will illustrate the sorts of decisions that a support group leader normally takes.

A group leader's diary

A consultant responsible for an infertility clinic recognized that many of the women attending the clinic found their situation quite distressing. Having attended a conference in which a paper was given outlining the use of support groups in an infertility clinic, he approached a social worker colleague with a request that she run a support group in his department on a trial basis. The group was advertised in the clinic and women attending for consultation and treatment were informed verbally. Attendance was, of course, optional. Eight decided to join the trial run of the group. Meetings were organized to be at monthly intervals with ten meetings in all.

The social worker had attended various groups during the course of the years but had led only one. Therefore, she decided to keep notes on her intentions for the group and record details of any significant events for discussion with her supervisor. It is helpful for us to review some of those records since they give the feel of the sorts of decisions which the leader was making and what sort of interventions resulted. We set out below the record of the first four meetings.

Meeting 1

Plan
My plan is to start on time with a warm greeting and then begin by looking through the short written introduction on the aims of the group. I will deal with any questions or confusions and then ask each member to introduce herself and take about three or four minutes to relate their situation. At the end of introductions I want to get a general discussion going and set them off getting to know each other. I will say something like, 'Well, we have half an hour left and we can use this time by saying anything further that has come to mind during the introductions or by asking each other about our lives in more detail.'

Outcome
In general, the first meeting went well. It seemed natural to suggest the introductions should follow round in a circle and since Adel, whom I know well as a confident young woman, was next to me, I asked her to start. Everybody followed in turn without fuss. Gill got a bit flustered and I helped her out by saying 'Take your time Gill – just tell us a little bit about yourself so that you are not a complete stranger.' The general discussion went with a swing and

quickly centred on their experiences at the clinic. Eventually the issue of problems in bringing husbands to the clinic was taken up. I did think of trying to deepen the discussion by saying 'How about our own problem in coming to the clinic?' but there was not much time left and it seemed a bit too heavy for the first meeting. I did notice that Gill and also Brenda said nothing further. I decided it was a relaxed atmosphere and to try and pull them into the discussion might have created tension. They seemed happy enough and laughed with the others. At the end, I asked them all to say how they felt about the first meeting and whether they would have second thoughts about coming next time. Everybody seemed positive.

Meeting 2

Plan

I hope that eventually we will get to exchanges which allow an expression of feelings concerning the problems they are having in getting pregnant and the possibility that they will never have children. I am aware that it is early for this so it must not be rushed. I plan to ask each member to begin by just saying what kind of a month they have had since we met – this is just as a warm-up and so that we can relearn names. Assuming that nothing of significance arises, I may well set a further cohesion-building task and suggest that we talk about 'how I cope on a bad day' (meaning when one is preoccupied with the thought of pregnancy or babies).

Outcome

Quite unexpected. Half-way through the warm-up Vicky began weeping (Maggie was just finishing talking at the time). I asked Vicky if she felt she would like to tell us what was affecting her. She said, with copious sobbing, that her husband had left her three days ago. Both I and the group were unprepared for this but we just naturally fell into supporting her and letting her talk. I let this run for 30 minutes and then became a little concerned that, although what we were doing was right, it would occupy the whole meeting. I did not know how several of the others were at the time and that bothered me. There seemed to be a slowing of the flood so I took the opportunity to say, 'Vicky, I think that we are all glad that you have trusted us enough to tell us what has happened and how you feel. I want to check how this is affecting everybody else here and also see how Dorothy, Ann and Liz are, because we have not heard from them yet. Does this feel OK to you?' This was fine with Vicky so I continued, 'We can't hear about such an awful experience without it affecting us so, for a moment, let's just talk about the feelings we had while we were listening to Vicky. Then we will check how the rest of us are generally.' This seemed to fit with the general mood. Two members (Adel and Liz) had found the event upsetting because it was a bit close to their own problems – but they were not distressed. As we wound down, I deliberately took the last word to reassure everybody that this was what support groups were for and Vicky came in to say that she was really grateful to have been able to talk it through.

Meeting 3

Plan

As always I will ask people to say how they are and then make it an open session to see what comes up.

Outcome

It was a fairly quiet meeting. Two of them were away. Vicky gave a quick summary of her situation and said that she did not want to be at the centre of today's meeting because, although she felt composed, she felt emotionally drained and just wanted to be in the company of the group without having to do or say much. Jenny wanted to talk about how tense she gets with internal examinations and this led to Ann getting angry about male consultants. It turned into a 'bash the consultants' session which was becoming un-productive. I intervened to ask 'Are the consultants that bad or are they convenient objects to get angry about? Is it possible that you are angry with your own bodies or even your husband's body because they will not produce a baby?' It did not work well and several of them came back with more horror stories to justify the anger. To end, because there was a sense of discord, I asked each member to say how they felt going home from a meeting and we shared the sense of being uplifted from being together.

Figure 16 Gaining a sense of uplift

Meeting 4

Plan
It will be an open session as before, with members taking a couple of minutes each at the beginning to say how they are.

Outcome
Everybody attended. The atmosphere was very flippant at first with Vicky recounting an 'offer made by a male friend in her time of need'. There seemed to be a reluctance to change the atmosphere into serious group work. I decided to let it run for a bit and sat quiet, although noticing that Ann was rather pensive and Gill seemed disapproving or embarrassed. After about ten minutes the jocular mood seemed to be running out of steam and I decided to take the chance and intervene to try and get us on to real work. I said, 'While we are in between stories I'd like to ask if anyone came to the group today with anything particular in their mind to discuss with us?' This certainly popped the bubble and there was a silence for a while. I did not speak further and finally Ann said she had thought about the last meeting a lot and maybe there was some truth in the fact that she resented her husband's problem (which she referred to as 'lazy sperm'). This led on to a really thrilling session in which most of the women truly talked of their feelings about their situation. There was a great deal of genuine disclosure and I barely needed to speak for much of the session – save giving an overview and ending the session. I felt that the group had moved on a stage and that the members had understood what being in a group was about.

The leader as the custodian of support group objectives

Having had the example of the infertility clinic showing the sort of thinking and decisions made by the leader of a typical support group (and noting, we hope, that her decisions were not based on rules or procedures but came from her sense of what felt right for the group at the time), it is appropriate now to brief you on the key principles which should guide your thinking and interventions as leader.

Even people with plenty of group experience and many hours of group work behind them can quite easily go off track and lose sight of their purpose and thus drift away from the required style of interaction needed in a support group. If this can happen to experienced group members, it will be even more likely for people in their first group, especially if the leader is unsure and does not intervene to restore direction. Thus, perhaps one of the most important duties on the part of the leader is to take a little time just before the beginning of each meeting to reflect on the contents and pattern of the previous

Figure 17 Losing sight of the purpose

meeting. Following this, it is worth taking the time to remind yourself of the objectives to be pursued in the group. These need to be kept clearly in mind throughout the ensuing meeting because your role is to develop a sense of whether or not the group is on target or off target in terms of the group objectives. Obviously, conversation in a group varies in character and intensity and time will inevitably be spent in catching up on news, joking, tension-relieving diversions, and so on. These are important in themselves as ways of building cohesion and maintaining a comfortable atmosphere. Intervention is only necessary if such exchanges are beginning to occupy a worrying amount of time and block effective work. In general, this monitoring style should be your basic strategy throughout any meeting of your group. That is, continually asking yourself, 'Is the group engaging in the type of work and conversation that we came here for? If not, is it because of a brief, unimportant allocation of time to alternative but acceptable activity or has the group become trapped in something which is way off track and is blocking effective work?' Should it be the latter, then you must, as leader, intervene in an attempt to redirect the group.

If you accept the recommendation to review your group's activity and atmosphere both before and during a meeting, some sort of framework will be helpful in order to keep things systematic – this is our next item. Incidentally, do remember that you do not have to bear this burden entirely alone. The group as a whole can be asked to take up the task. It is a useful move which can lead to productive discussion and learning.

A framework for reviewing a support group meeting

Safety – Does the support group seem safe for the members?

Many of the vital ingredients of a successful support group will wither and die if you do not maintain a sense of safety in your group. The attempt to build cohesion and a sense of belonging, and also to foster self-exploration through self-disclosure is hopeless if the members do not feel safe. Naturally, some people will feel insecure and threatened because they bring this through the door with them as part of an enduring character. However, even relatively robust people will be withdrawn and defensive if they sense that something is making the group unsafe.

How can this be judged? In a support group the members will, ideally, gain a sense of uplift as a result of attending a meeting. If, however, your whole group or, more likely, individual members are on the receiving end of experiences which produce anger, acute tension, embarrassment or a sense of being 'forcibly' psychologically exposed, then the outcome will be the opposite of uplifting. It is a delicate balance that has to be achieved. The members have joined the group to do psychological work. The group is clearly failing if, in the attempt to avoid difficult issues, the meeting is reduced to tea and giggles because of an over-protective leader. The group tasks and your invitation to participate should pose a gentle challenge. Similarly the way you 'model' openness and reciprocal supportiveness with a clear invitation to follow suit also poses a challenge. However, while this challenge will probably be valued by the members (since they will have brought expectations of the group as something new that leads somewhere), it is easily undermined if involvement in early exchanges is experienced as traumatic or attacking. Your greatest aid in discovering whether or not this is the case is to ask individual members how they are feeling. Clearly you cannot be doing this every 5 minutes but if ever there is doubt, do not hesitate because the very act of your inquiry re-establishes an atmosphere of care and concern together with a reminder that you, the leader, are there as a safety net. This point will now be illustrated with some commonly occurring situations which threaten group safety.

Attempts at 'forcible psychological exposure'

The following sequence speaks for itself. The group was composed of teachers who had requested help in setting up a support and interpersonal growth group. The membership had therefore chosen itself. After several efforts at pseudo self-disclosure, one member in particular had taken to urging other members to follow his lead, thereby creating some discomfort for them:

Mark: Well, I don't know why we are wasting so much time sitting round in silence – some folks are not pulling their weight. We all know what we are here for, it's been explained well enough. Some of us have made the effort – what about some action out of the rest of you?

Maggie: Do stop being so pushy, Mark, not everybody wants to jump into it with two big flat feet. (*laughter*)

Mark: That's all very well but I don't intend to keep giving up two hours which I can't really spare if nothing is going to happen.

Alan: I think that he has got a point. How about hearing something from the women? Most of you have barely said a word.

Mark: (*Sensing an ally and instantly teaming up*) Yes, that's right. Come on, then, Angela, what about you, it must be your turn. Get yourself into the hot seat – it doesn't really hurt. Alan and I have survived.

Angela: Why pick on me? I don't feel ready.

Mark: Oh, come on, we're all friends here, we're not going to eat you. Take the plunge, the water is nice when you get in. Tell us why you have been so quiet this term. What has been upsetting you?

Leader: I must make a comment before Angela replies, if she wishes to reply, that is. I think that it is right that we should talk through the point about participation. We are all responsible for our own participation and therefore should all be involved in considering it, but we must decide for ourselves when to make a personal contribution, it should not be decided by another member, not in a support group like this. One of our most important targets had to be that of trusting each other. So I would like us to think about the last minute or so of our conversation and what sort of feelings it led to. Mark has been trying to persuade Angela to talk about herself. He has used words like 'hot seat' and 'not really hurting' which seem rather threatening to me. Perhaps one of our problems is that not everybody feels safe to participate. I would like to ask each of you in turn how safe do you feel here and if you do not feel that safe can you try and express what it is that takes away the safety?

This was, of course, a very directive intervention on the part of the leader. He explained it by saying that he felt Angela was being manoeuvred into a position of enforced self-disclosure which might have been very traumatic for her. She had been very reserved and was obviously distressed by something. She needed a greater level of trust than was available in the group at that time. Furthermore, the leader felt that the reception any significant disclosure would receive might also be damaging since the group had been slow to develop cohesion and was not yet equipped to deal with overt emotional reaction of sensitive personal issues. He judged it necessary to intervene in order to deflect pressure from Angela. The intervention brought about a brief halt, thus giving the group the opportunity to look at what was going on and learn more about what safety in a group entails. Thus, the leader headed off a damaging incident and turned the occasion into a gentle learning experience which improved the group atmosphere. In other types of group the leader might take a much more 'hands off' approach. In a support group, though, this is not appropriate. The leader must act to conserve safety when it is seriously under threat. It is not possible to give exact criteria as to when this is necessary, this has to be a matter for your own judgement. In general, though, do not overdo it. An over-protective leader is a considerable impediment to group development.

Badly handled disclosure and emotional expression

A member of a group takes risks when overcoming natural reticence and telling those present of very personal and, possibly, feeling-laden aspects of their life. In the immediate moment of disclosure people can and do feel extraordinary vulnerable. If the disclosure has provoked strong feeling, tears perhaps, then the member may also feel rather 'emotionally naked'. In a close, tolerant, understanding and supportive atmosphere the member's vulnerability will be sensed and the group will instinctively collaborate in making a special effort to help the member. This is not about tidying away the emotion or moving on to less uncomfortable issues. Quite the opposite. It is about getting closer – often literally physically closer, in order to give physical contact and the sense of a close-knit centre of support. The member may then be encouraged to take all the time needed to continue with what is being shared or to cry his or her tears without inhibition.

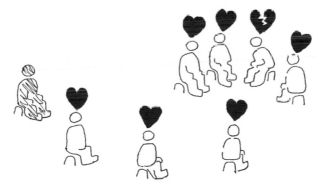

Figure 18 Emotionally naked

The inexperienced group may handle such events badly at first. This is especially likely if there are people present who are frightened of expressing their own feelings since this means that they are usually bothered by others expressing their feelings too. Sometimes a group can become paralysed in an awful, immobile and embarrassed silence. Alternatively, the member's contribution may be 'passed over'. As leader you will help a great deal by modelling how to deal with disclosure and emotional expression. Your target is to relax the atmosphere, give permission both to the individual involved and the group that it is right to continue and create a shared feeling of safety. Two moments from separate groups illustrate the sort of intervention a leader might make.

A member of a support group for psychiatric nurses has been talking about a visit he had made to see his mother who had been taken into a hospice:

> *Don*: Actually, the ward had a really nice atmosphere. I've done some time in oncology myself and I must say that this was far better than the ward I worked on.
>
> *Nita*: Was your mother pleased to see you? I remember you saying that you don't get on that well.
>
> *Don*: Oh, yes, it was OK, no problem at all really. She didn't have much energy but she was quite with it. I guess she did not have energy for nagging. She wanted to talk about Dad. He died three years ago and it was a great shock to us all. We . . . my mother and me . . . never really talked about it. They all sort of looked to me as the one to have the strength and give the support. Nobody ever asked me what I felt about it.
>
> *Leader*: What were those feelings, Don?
>
> *Don*: (*Long pause*) I missed him more than I thought possible . . . we were always such good friends. (*voice broken*) He was so . . . sorry. (*Don can no longer talk. He hides his face in his hands, he is visibly crying*).

The group is silent, the members seem tense and unsure, momentarily Don is alone with his grief.

> *Leader*: Nita, Paul, give Don some physical support will you? Move closer and put your arm around him. Let's all try and give Don some back-up, move your chair closer in if you can. Don we are all with you . . . try and relax with us, you've got all the time in the world. Tell us about the images of your father which came to mind and put you in touch with your grief.

The group spent another 30 minutes helping Don express his grief. One other member was also moved to tears and was similarly supported without deflecting attention from Don. Through this incident the members were shown that living and expressing feeling in the presence of the group members is an important and safe part of group work. They felt the relaxed confidence of the leader in accepting the emotion. They saw how he greeted it with increased physical contact and a shift into a specially focused and very gentle period of work solely with Don. Later, as Don surfaced from these feelings, the leader checked around generally about what the other members were feeling and how they had been affected by Don's experiences. The members learned that there was nothing to fear and much to gain in expressing feeling and supporting one another while so doing. As is typical, this particular group rapidly learned to handle such moments with ease and the direct intervention of the leader was no longer needed to see them through.

The second example was an incident which occurred in a group which had met six times and thus was not wholly unused to group interaction and disclosure. However, they seemed caught off guard by a disclosure from one of the members and came close to abandoning him without response to it – an event which could well have caused him real psychological damage. Each member had, in turn, spoken briefly saying how they were and whether there was any need on their part to have some time in the group that day to deal with personal issues. The personal statements had been unexceptional until Andrew spoke.

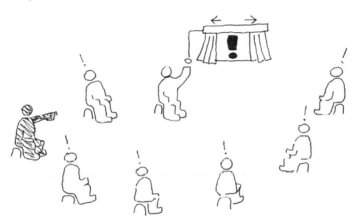

Figure 19 A disclosure

> *Andrew*: It has been a really difficult week for me. I have agonized at great length on whether I should tell you about it. I decided last night that I should. So I am declaring that I need some time this week please. I won't keep you in suspense either . . . we had a young lad in the unit last week, about 18 years old. It has totally shaken me because I've realized that I have become very attached to him. Too attached really. It could easily become an obsession. So I've been thinking the obvious – I don't know if I'm homosexual.

As with the previous incident, this disclosure took the group unawares and for a while they floundered with it. No reply was made for some moments and an awkward silence developed. In some circumstances it would be appropriate for a leader to let the silence run on and thus allow the group to learn a coping style of its own. However, in this instance the psychological safety of a member was at some risk and the leader, quite sensibly, decided to intervene in order to make sure that the disclosure did not lead to embarrassment, rejection or isolation. The group was young and inexperienced and had not found its feet with very personal issues such as this. The leader was also aware of the need to make this a moment for learning, thus fostering confidence and skill in handling such instances within the group:

> *Leader*: I'm glad that you trusted us sufficiently to share this with us, Andrew. Tell us how you feel at this exact moment.
>
> *Andrew*: Well . . . OK, I suppose. I'm glad I got it out – but it has gone a bit quiet round here. That's a bit unnerving.
>
> *Leader*: (*To the group*) At a time like this it is vital that we give one another full support, it can be alarming to have shared something very personal and have that followed by a silence. It is hard to know what people are thinking. As Andrew says, it is unnerving. Try to remember that we do not have to solve each other's problems. We are here really to provide a place to express them and help each other think them through. So try to respond immediately and simply at times like this. It is quite useful to just feedback what your initial reactions have been . . . maybe we could have a go at doing that now so that Andrew can feel drawn back in?
>
> *Dave*: Alright – I'll start. I'm sorry to have left you in the lurch, as it were, Andrew. I felt it was a tremendous step for you to say that and I admire you for it. I don't know what I think about it yet. In one way I couldn't care less. In another, it clearly causes you much concern so I'm bothered for you. But basically – surprise, I suppose I don't really believe it.

Then followed an intense but supportive discussion involving most of the members. At the next meeting Andrew reported that he had gone home feeling fine after these exchanges and felt no worry about the reception of his disclosure. He felt well received and valued within the group.

In these examples the leader was not putting words into the members' mouths or manipulating the group. Rather, an invitation was given to handle things in a particular way. This invitation was delivered at a time when the group seemed lost and likely to do unintended damage. The interventions were both to protect the individual member from the inexperience of the group generally, and also to guarantee the very basic commodity of a successful support group, that is, safety. At the same time there was an element of tutoring going on. Rather than leaving the members unsure and confused, the leader passed on experience from former groups, thereby helping the members to grow in ability at group work.

Problematic silences

From time to time a group will fall silent. In a 'mature' group a silence may last for several minutes. This will not be a tense time with people wracking their brain for something to say. The members will use it as an opportunity for introspection and reflection, asking themselves the questions 'Where are my thoughts? What feelings am I aware of? What is my immediate awareness of myself and the group? What do I have to say to any of the other members of the group – about them or about me?'

Silences are not threatening if they are seen as an alternative way of being together and working at a common task. It can be especially relaxing to experience silences in a group in which trust and tolerance have developed and with this the knowledge that, during silences, the members are taking time to look within themselves, but at the same time are still drawing on the companionship of the group. Thus, before long at least one person will know that they have uncovered the next item of group business and the group will spring to life again.

Having made this point, it also has to be said that in the early meetings silences are not always an indication of this reflective activity. Nor are they necessarily comfortable and relaxing. Therefore, in your role as leader, you must judge whether the early silences are 'good' silences or whether they are motivated by tension, resentment, confusion or some similar problem. For example, events of the type described above may raise tension and cause the members to retreat into a protective silence. Angry outbursts can have the same effect. More likely, in early meetings a group can find itself finishing with one person's material and then being unsure as to 'what next' If the group is still unbalanced in that some members are talkers and some have yet to find confidence and so hang back, then there may be a silence that is about pressurizing the less active members into being more forthcoming. Such silences are often tense and counter-productive since the members who lack confidence will feel even less confident in the situation and retreat further into their shell.

In short, there is more than one kind of silence. The meaning attached to the silence and the internal activity that accompanies it are therefore matters of judgement. In deciding whether or not a silence is a good silence or one in which you, the leader, should take the initiative to help the group move on, you are dependent on your sense of what the atmosphere is about and how this relates to what has gone on before. If the members seem stuck, tense and unsure then from the point of view of preserving safety it is as well to help them out, for example:

> *Leader:* Everybody seems very absorbed in thought – try and make the effort to surface these thoughts and share them with everybody.

or:

> *Leader:* I just want to check with you what is going on and what is occupying your attention at the moment – we have been silent for several minutes. It is good to be silent for a while now and again to think a little and decide how we are feeling about things. At the same time don't forget our group contract – to make the effort to voice what it is that we are feeling, even if that is just that we are feeling unsure.

In deciding if you are going to intervene to end a silence, there are some important issues to bear in mind. Check initially on your own motive and how this links to your own feeling. Is a silence making you tense, and is it your need to end it that is putting you under pressure? If so, what is bothering you about the silence? This, ideally, is something to work out with your supervisor if you have one. Perhaps you are being over-protective? Perhaps in your anxiety to make the group a success you cannot give the group space to have quiet periods or 'flat spots'? Maybe you want to rush them into maturity with meaningful and rich conversation filling most of the time? In other words, do not rush to take over in a silence. Silences are normal and productive group behaviour if they are working silences and lead on to useful exchanges. Your aim must be to help the group develop the capacity to use and tolerate silences. The worst thing to do is to create a situation in which the group starts to expect an intervention from you every time there is a brief pause. Intervene only when you think that the essential sense of safety is at risk for some members, or when you feel that the silence is for negative reasons, is going nowhere, and could be turned into a useful opportunity for tutoring the group into more effective behaviour.

Disruptive or unsuitable members

Obviously, despite the best of intentions and efforts at selection, it does happen that a group ends up with a member who is not suited to the activity. In our own experience this has happened with such a low frequency that we are tempted to describe it as a rare event. However, if you are in a situation where there is no control over selection, or if selection has proved to be inadequate, then it could become rather more common.

The most likely problem in the client or staff support group which we have in mind is that of a person who has limited contact with his or her own feeling life. Early on he or she will find the effort of the group to make contact with and share feelings highly threatening. In efforts to dispel the threat, disruption may ensue.

For example, a group for mixed hospital staff designed both for support and personal training ran into difficulties during its first meeting. A young administrator began to make remarks which distracted the group and undermined the group leader. The following exchange took place after about one hour:

John: (*After a brief group silence*) This really is a total waste of time and a bore. We might just as well be in the pub – discuss work problems over a jar. Come on, Alison (*the group leader*) give us a clue what are we supposed to be talking about.

Leader: The idea is, as you know, that we do not have a fixed agenda. Each member is responsible for their own contribution. Try to look back over recent days and identify issues which have provoked some feeling in you and share these with the group.

John: I'm not into all this feeling stuff. Quite frankly, I think it is a load of crap. Things are best dealt with rationally. What is the point of stirring everybody up like this? What we need is a bit of fun, that is the best way to deal with stress in my view, not sitting around looking for things to be sorry for yourself over and then wallowing in it.

Leader: Are there people in your life that you do talk with about your inner feelings, John?

John: No way, lady – you are not pulling me into it like that. In fact, I think I've had enough of this. I regard it as futile. You can all waste an hour if you can afford it, but I've got more important things to do. See you around. (*John leaves the room, slamming the door.*)

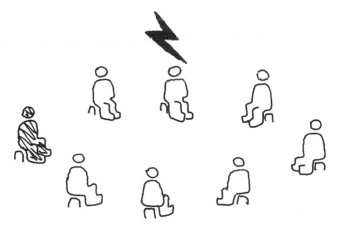

Figure 20 A member who is not suited to the activity

Quite why John ever joined this group is far from clear. Since the pre-group briefing was carried out adequately he knew the manner in which the group would be conducted. At least, he ought to have known. Possibly he blocked off the real implication of the information he received because he was highly motivated to attend for other reasons. Be that as it may, the incident illustrates how these things can and do crop up. Fortunately perhaps, this leader did not have to take any strenuous steps to resolve the problem. John resolved it himself by leaving, though it did leave the group and its leader having to deal with the anger and hostility left behind. Our personal experience with groups has been on similar lines. In the rare event of a member being unsuited to a group to a degree that he or she cannot participate in a way which is congruent with the general objectives, then the member usually becomes so uncomfortable that the problem is solved by their leaving. At one level this is a cause for relief, although it is of course sad for the individual concerned since the opportunity for developing the ability to contact and work with feelings is then lost.

Other forms of actual disruption (as distinct from people having problems with the group situation) are even more rare. Support groups may disappoint in that it can take a long while for some members to make effective use of the group and truly commit themselves to its activity. Defensive patterns such as excessive jocularity may intrude but the timely intervention of the leader will usually be more than sufficient to contain the problem. If in doubt, simply point out to the group what you see happening, indicate why this is disadvantageous, and let the group decide on the issue. Take care though, not to do this in a way which appears to be punishing or blaming.

What if John had not left and remained as a perpetually disturbing presence? Almost always the group pressure to conform and allow other members to use the group opportunity as they wish will win the day. It may not happen instantly, but other members will begin to feel angry towards members like John because little can develop with such destructive interjections and the sense of cooperating together is broken up. On occasions, members who are initially quite disturbing to a group will be positively influenced by group pressure and later become effective participants – by far the best outcome. Very rarely, the disruptive member may have such a strong personality, and such fixed views, that they influence weaker members unduly, and seek to build up their own 'gang' within the group, maybe even try to take it over altogether. It's important that any such behaviour be spotted sooner rather than later, and some attempt made to counteract such pressures. This would be an excellent opportunity for the leader's consultant/supervisor to show their mettle, and shows how necessary it can be to provide oneself with such professional support.

Thus, overall, the message must be – allow things to unfold but keep a careful check on whether or not a disruptive member is doing serious damage to the group. If so, intervene to point this out and, in the first instance, help him or her out as best you can. Remember that the disruptive activity may be a way of expressing tension or testing limits and it may subside with caring leadership. In the extreme (and we have never known this to be necessary) the group leader may decide that the group cannot continue with the member attending. For example, if a member continually arrives drunk and incapable of participating properly, this cannot be allowed to continue. At least two courses are open. First, the leader may take the member aside individually and make the request that they stop attending, giving clear reasons why and, possibly, a route back into the group. Second, the leader can make it a group issue and a group decision. This perhaps is a harder course for the individual concerned since it leads, effectively, to a rejection by the whole group – not a nice experience. The ideal is for the disruptive member to come to see that the group is not for them, then they can make the decision to withdraw.

Anger

The point has been made several times that the approach adopted in a support group differs from that of other types of group. Each has their own style according to objective, emphasis and limits. In certain types of group, for example those with a Kleinian group analytic style, anger has a central place. The group experience is, in part, structured to enable members to discover their anger and the circumstances which provoke it. We (the authors) have both encountered a situation in which tension was created in a support group because one or more members had a background in Kleinian-style group work. Their 'instinct' was to work towards uncovering and expressing anger. However, this clashed with the basic objective of safety and cohesion. These are the things which have to be guaranteed in a support group, and although working with anger is not of necessity destructive of them, it can put them at risk. *If a person attends a group session feeling fragile, in need of support and hopeful of going away with that sense of uplift which good support can give, yet finds that they are disturbed and ruffled by an unexpected expression of anger directed to them, then the opposite of support is taking place.*

This reveals a dilemma in support work. It is not psychologically advantageous to suppress anger. Unexpressed anger will often be converted into behaviour which 'sours' the atmosphere of a group session in subtle ways. At the same time certain expressions of anger can alter the sense of cohesion in a group quite dramatically. Similarly, anger can reduce the supportive power of a session to zero and distract the group. A further problem arises with groups composed of people who have to work with each other after the meetings. The upset of an angry confrontation will have difficult repercussions later on in the work setting unless it is well handled and properly resolved.

It must be stressed at this point that the problem we are focused upon is to do with anger between members and not an individual member expressing anger related to a personal issue which they are presenting to the group.

The underlying theme of this section is that the leader must act as the custodian of the group objectives. The implication here is that, as leader, you are faced with some difficult decisions should your group arrive at a position where anger is being directed from one member to another. In our view the best course is to take appropriate opportunities to remind members of the central importance of cohesion and support. However, if issues to do with anger do arise, show the group how to deal with it in a manner which minimizes the threat to the group cohesion. This takes us into what is best called the *constructive expression of anger*. To a point, this involves talking of anger rather than being openly angry with someone. It is a way of signalling anger and dealing with the underlying cause in order to resolve the anger and become free of it. We will illustrate this by two brief exchanges based on an actual incident.

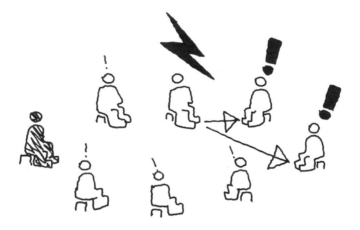

Figure 21 Unmodified anger

Unmodified anger

A group is in the middle of a meeting where there has been an exchange on the theme of difficult colleagues. The group has fallen into a brief silence:

> *Ian:*   Anybody put anything on the Grand National then?
> *Rod:*   Well, I quite fancied Crystal Girl myself.
> *Ian:*   Crystal Girl – no chance.
> *Rod:*   Oh, I don't know, worth giving it a go, a lot of potential there on the right day.
> *Gillian:*   For Christ's sake. What do you think this is? If you are both so

immature that you can't see how inappropriate and pathetic this is, then you have no place in a group like this – it is supposed to be for adults.

Stunned silence follows.

The constructive expression of anger
Assume that the exchange between Ian and Rod has been ongoing just as above. How might Gillian have both signalled that she found this very facile and annoying yet, at the same time, retained a bond of closeness with her two fellow members and left a good working atmosphere intact?

Gillian: I want to say something to Ian and Rod. I know that you are just relaxing together with this chatter about the horse race but I can't cope with it today. I can feel myself getting really angry with you. I could throw something at you both, to be honest. I know I'm going a bit over the top. I feel cross out of proportion to the event because you are not usually like this.

Ian: Oh – sorry about that, I suppose it was a bit indulgent. I guess it has been a long day and I'm feeling like winding down.

Gillian: Well, it's alright – but I did need to tell you that I was feeling pretty cross. It seemed so inappropriate to be discussing horses in the middle of a group.

Leader: Just let me pick you up on one thing which you said Gillian. You remarked that you were feeling anger which was out of proportion to the event. Perhaps we should look at the situation and see if it reminds you of something elsewhere.

Gillian: (*After thought*) I get really disappointed in the staff room. The talk is so superficial. If one tries to begin a conversation of any depth it is ruined by idiot males who have to turn everything into a cheap joke, or talk mindlessly about sport. I often feel the same kind of anger as just now. It can be so frustrating and so lonely there at times.

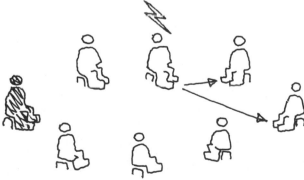

Figure 22 Constructive anger

Thus, in the first example the explosion of anger was disruptive and shocked the group, making relationships very strained for some while. The alternative way allowed an expression of anger which preserved relationships and led on to some effective personal work. The group 'grew' as a result. As leader, you should consider both modelling and teaching this approach, which allows anger to be included and dealt with in a support-style group without disturbing the all-important level of safety.

A final point on this theme of anger and safety. We have tried to illustrate the fact that group process does, at times, lead to angry feelings. Further, in your role as leader, it will be helpful if you gently steer your group so that the way in which such anger is expressed leads on to effective work and group growth. Do not, however, become phobic of angry exchange within the group. If it does occur, think carefully before immediately rushing to damp down an expression of anger, the group may be quite capable of dealing with it without your help. In fact, some members may well find repeated interventions to head off anger frustrating and angering in itself. You will get to know your group quite quickly and will soon have a sense of what it can cope with and what it needs help with (bearing in mind the comments above concerning a leader's motives for intervention). Furthermore, you will also find that many groups eventually develop a powerful capacity for self-healing.

In the first incident a quiet and calming word from the leader would, most likely, set in motion self-healing processes, for example:

> *Leader:*   Gillian, that was a rather unusual moment for you. It will be a help to all of us if you will talk it through with us. Why did you find Ian and Rod's chatter so annoying? Try and rework the situation – what you were thinking and feeling? See if these remind you of things outside the group.

Anger towards the leader

Most people who lead support groups do so because they have a caring concern for their clients and colleagues. This may also combine with a personal need for the cohesion and intimacy which groups usually provide. Rarely will the leader of a support group consciously behave in a way which provokes anger. Despite this, the leader can attract anger and you will be wise to 'budget' for this and accept it as part of a relatively predictable group process. By what mechanism does it come about?

Members may 'project' responsibility onto the leader for making the group a good group, rather than seeing that it is primarily their own responsibility to bear. If the atmosphere of a group goes through a 'flat patch', disappointment can provoke a subdued, angry frustration and the leader may well find him or herself somewhat embattled for a while as this anger becomes directed at him or her. If, therefore, you unexpectedly find yourself absorbing complaints about the group generally, its purpose, the procedures used, inadequacies (e.g., 'we never get angry with one another') and so on, it may be that you are being used as an object on which to offload frustration. Your own feelings are a useful guide in these circumstances. If you feel a sense of indignation and injustice, a sense of 'Where has this come from? I don't deserve this. Why are they getting at me?' the diagnosis may fit (always bearing in mind that sometimes leaders can obstruct group functioning and provoke justified anger). In the event, be open and honest; tell the group of your feelings of injustice and lead the way into a discussion about where the anger and complaining has come from. This should result in a review of problems within the group and a reminder about members taking personal responsibility for making it work along the lines of the contract.

Self-disclosure by the leader

As leader of a support group you are also part of the group. You must never abandon that bit of yourself which is watching, considering and caring for the members, but at the same time do not take the leadership role to extremes. You are not there to be a cold automaton, a rock of resolve and inscrutable calm, far from it. The group exists to encourage the release and expression of emotion and this will be impeded by a leader who maintains a lofty remoteness. Such a stance threatens safety ('He takes it all in with those cold, cod fish eyes. It makes you feel like you are being judged all the time. I hate it') and may eventually distract the group. Some types of group (again the group analytic type as described, for example, by Hyde (1988)) operate on the basis that the leader is present simply to interpret group dynamics. Inscrutable remoteness is considered to be an essential aid to this objective. It is characteristic of this mechanical behaviour, for example, that the leader keeps rigid timing and will get up and leave at the scheduled end of the session even if a member is in the middle of one of the most important statements she has ever made. The support group leader has differing objectives and therefore is present in the group as a living and breathing human being. Be involved with your group, empathize with them. Laugh with them or be sad with them. Above all, be a real person with them. This is all perfectly possible without surrendering your role and presence as the leader.

There are limits though. If you are a professional care-giver running a group for clients who are involved in some common, distressing situation, then it is obvious that the group is for their benefit. It would be inappropriate for you, as leader, to use their time to deal with your own personal issues. It would certainly be difficult for the group members if you became involved to the point of losing emotional control yourself, thus needing to be cared for by the members. Once more, this is a potential means of losing safety and the best course is to be involved, but retain your identity as leader and not as client. Be careful to avoid having the tables turned, with the group seeking to make you their patient, perhaps with the best of intentions.

According to the terms of operation, a staff support group may offer more freedom for the leader to function as a participant. This applies particularly where the group members are well experienced in group work and have a professional background such as counselling. Sometimes leaders are designated 'participant leaders' indicating that, to a limited degree, they will be forthcoming with personal reaction and feeling to other group members and also with reference to personal issues of their own. This has to be a limited involvement though, as when presenting personal issues the leader's attention is no longer focused on the needs of the group – in other words, it has briefly become a leaderless group and this may threaten safety. Unless that is, you have made provision for a co-group leader (as is described in the next section) or, with a mature group, the members can temporarily look after the basic leadership themselves.

The use of a co-leader

A co-leader is a group member and normal participant who takes on two additional functions. First, the co-leader gives the leader feedback and comment after a meeting. Basically, this is a supportive event for the leader and offers an opportunity to see the events of a meeting from a different perspective. It also gives the leader a chance to explore ideas and concerns related to the group. Second, if an occasion arises wherein the leader needs to do some personal work, then an arrangement can be made at the time, with the consent of the group, for the co-leader to take over as temporary leader. This then avoids the problem of the group becoming leaderless. Even with this facility there are, in our view, still limits in terms of self-disclosure which the leader should not exceed. Any disclosures which threaten the group's sense of trust and reliance on the leader also threaten safety. They therefore belong in another place.

In general, the use of a co-group leader is recommended. If you decide to introduce the practice, choose someone whose judgement you trust and make an arrangement in a common-sense way. It has to be someone who can comment intelligently on the events of the group meetings and act as a sounding board for your ideas. Therefore, choose someone with previous group experience if possible. As a safeguard it is important that you and your co-leader should openly talk out and resolve the issue of competitive feelings. Without this there may be conflicting interpretations of the things that happen within the group or, worse, a discernible tension between you both which the members will pick up.

Visitors

Sometimes people ask if they can visit a group. Quite often this sort of request will come from people in authority who have a need to keep control. In general, a visitor will cripple a group meeting if the group is of a closed membership type and has built up a sense of intimacy and trust. On grounds of safety the circumstance is best avoided unless the group has discussed it and agreed to allow it. For groups with a transient membership, visitors are usually less of a threat and, if forewarned and given a chance to consider it, such a group may be able to accommodate a visitor without too much disruption.

Identifying and understanding patterns within the support group

As we have already mentioned in Chapter 4 and as you will rapidly discover, the patterns of interaction in a group can be varied and complex. While not wishing to be depressing, we have to say that the ability to identify and understand these patterns in full cannot be learned through reading a few pages of an introductory text like this. Such learning comes from hundreds of hours of time spent in groups combined with some form of apprenticeship-style tuition. What we can reasonably offer, though, is a brief review of the types of phenomena that go under the title of 'group dynamics', together with some general principles which you ought to bear in mind when trying to understand events in your group. As a result, you may be able to recognize some of the things which we describe, and this ability will, hopefully, give you further confidence in running your group.

The concept of group dynamics

As we have already advised, it is an important and worthwhile practice at the end of each separate meeting of a group to think through the general flow of events in the meeting and to try and account for what happened. For example, you may be able to notice that some issues will have been readily accepted by the group as a topic for sharing and discussion while others will have been rejected by one means or another, almost as if there were prior agreement.

Similarly, if you think about the part which each member played in the meeting, it may emerge that some members took a clear role which almost merited a title, e.g. the group patient, the group parent or the group spokesman, and that the rest of the group fitted in with this assumption of role. In fact, the other members may have had more to do with the development of the pattern than was immediately obvious, since a group may 'collaborate' in making the roles available and locking willing participants into them.

It is important to be clear exactly how we are using this term 'collaborates'. It is not to imply that there has been rational discussion and some kind of collective agreement – the opposite in fact. The implication is that a sense of collective agreement and cooperation to achieve a common end came about without the members having conscious awareness of what was happening and probably without their being able to see it until it was pointed out. This idea that people in a group may function together to produce a particular situation without an immediate awareness of so doing is the very core of the theory of group dynamics. Bion (1961) was among the first to write about this phenomenon. From his experiences with psychotherapy groups he believed that there existed a 'collective unconscious'. Throughout the life of the group its members would, at times, function together to achieve ends related to three shared sets of feelings and needs. These were described as *dependency* – the need to find a leader or some means of safety and protection; *fight or flight* – collective responses to perceived threats to security in the group; and *pairing* – the formation of alliances within the group which again gives increased comfort in the face of threat. In this theory the idea of threat is related to things which make people uncomfortable, for example, the expression of feelings or the distortion of the group by a member who constantly bids for attention.

Several theorists have put forward competing explanatory models of group dynamics equivalent to that of Bion but we will not try to discuss them all here. Hyde (1988) gives a useful overview with a helpful bibliography for further reading. Perhaps two approaches which do merit specific mention in relation to our purposes here (because of their practical spirit) are the ideas of Whitaker and Lieberman (1964) and, although in great contrast, those of Eric Berne (1966).

Whitaker and Lieberman introduced the so-called *focal conflict* model of group functioning. The basic assumption is that although members arrive at a group as individuals, they become part of a collective psychology such that all share in the emergence of 'group themes'. As Hyde (1988) puts it:

> Group members are invited to discuss their concerns, whatever is important to them. Open discussion develops, and there is a flow of associations from the different members. Each member only responds to part of what has previously been said, and participates verbally or silently, by being attentive or inattentive, sprawled out, restless or tense. As the conductor [leader] listens to these interactions, in time a theme emerges. The group theme has some relevance to all the group, each responding individually to the theme, as it

arouses thoughts and feelings specific to that individual's past and present experience.

Thus, for example, a support group for teachers had fallen into the pattern of checking around its members at the beginning of a meeting to establish who, if anyone, had a particular problem for which they wished to use group time. On their eleventh meeting three members had indicated that they had significant issues which they hoped to present. One of these members, Liz, was a 35-year-old single woman who had told the group a little while back that she might have a medical problem and was booked to visit a surgeon. Liz was in a sombre mood. The group thus sensed that she had visited her surgeon and that it was bad news. At least two of the other members knew from individual conversations that she had a breast lump and might, therefore, have to lose the breast. The significance of this for a single woman of 35 was, naturally, disturbing to them and to the others in the group who had a fairly shrewd idea of what the problem was. About two-thirds of the group were women.

After the customary, initial 'group round' to establish who wanted group time (i.e. each member took a few minutes to say how they were and whether or not they wanted some time to talk through anything with the group), the next task was to sort out when each of the three would present their material. Liz hung back and ended up being the last of the three in order. The group was accepting of the situation. The first in order presented material which, while not a directly personal problem, had relevance to all the teachers present – a case of child sexual abuse. This led to a lengthy discussion and consumed an hour of the group's one and a half hours. Prompted by the leader, the group recognized this and scurried on to the next issue. The second in order presented a personal problem caused by a dementing elderly parent. The group had always agreed that strict time-keeping was essential and that they had to finish promptly at 6 p.m. It was therefore at ten minutes to six that, apologetically, the group turned to Liz and asked her if she felt she could make any use of the remaining time. Liz, rather hurt and dispirited, said that there was no point and that maybe she would talk about it another time or perhaps deal with it on a one-to-one basis elsewhere. The other members expressed great guilt about having let Liz down.

What had happened here? These were kindly, supportive people who would not have wanted to let Liz down. The problem was the very lengthy discussion on child sexual abuse and the teachers' response to this. The leader, himself a teacher but with some group experience, had let this run on, apparently as involved as the rest of the group in the theme.

An interpretation of the turn of events in this meeting was greatly helped by the concept of a group theme. What was the theme of this meeting though – how was it decided? Basically we have to examine what was set before the group and what challenge this posed. Then, taking an overview, we ask how the group spent its time and whether there appeared to be a consistent pattern which involved most, or all, of the members. The knowledge that Liz might have bad news was clearly placed before the group and it must have been recognized by most members that it could be quite traumatic going through it with her. This may not have been a conscious thought though. In response to the request by Liz for some time the group certainly agreed and wanted to help her with the issue. However, an 'accident' occurred. The group became preoccupied with something else and lost track of the time. The content of the preoccupying conversation was probably less important than the fact that it occurred (although it is of interest that it was to do with child abuse, that is the violation of a person's body – close, in a sense, to the problem that Liz was facing). The group theme, therefore, may well have been 'become busily engaged in something else to avoid the pain and trauma of Liz's fright and grief'. This would have been in the form of a shared need that did not reach conscious awareness but, nevertheless, directed the behaviour of the members.

Within the terms of Whitaker and Lieberman's theory, the behaviour of the group would be seen as a solution to a 'focal conflict'. The elements of the conflict are fairly obvious. The members wished to help Liz but, at the same time, were wary of the consequences of beginning because of what they might have to face. The solution to the conflict was to be busily engaged on other things. This was not hostile but a defence against the possibility of being overwhelmed by powerful feelings. If someone had stopped the meeting to inquire what was going on, it is unlikely that any of the members could have accounted for the event in these terms though. At the time it would have felt like being interested in the other topic and losing track of time. The most important aspect is that it was a collective experience, the feelings were felt by all and they all cooperated (including Liz) to achieve the outcome, that is avoiding exposure to Liz's trauma. Whitaker (1985) gives a very clear and helpful explanation of this approach, classifying group solutions as either *restrictive*, where effective work is blocked and *enabling*, where the group deals with key issues openly and effectively.

As you must realize, this was an interpretation of a group dynamic and, like all such interpretations is best seen as an aid to understanding possibilities rather than cold fact. To learn more about this style of accounting for group patterns, have a look at the original work (given above) and Whitaker (1985). Alternatively, Hyde (1988) gives a concise but useful summary.

Our last presentation of the key ideas of a theorist takes us to Eric Berne. His name became well known many years ago following the publication of *Games People Play* (1964). Following on from the discussion so far the central notion of his theory has a familiar ring. He argued that many transactions between people were governed by motives and objectives that were not known to the people at a conscious level. Often the circumstances of these transactions became repetitious and therefore 'ritualized' a proportion of what went on between two or more people – the origin of the so-called 'game'. From this theory there developed a technique of therapy which was conducted in group form and is now well established as *Transactional Analysis*. Berne (1966) gives the general approach to running TA groups. It is a worthwhile book in terms of helping someone who is not familiar with group dynamics to build up a greater understanding of the breadth of the phenomena. At times you may find it useful to reflect whether or not your group is involved in a collective game, or whether some members (including yourself) may use game strategies to achieve an objective within the group:

Case study The group game

A support group of professional therapists had been in existence for some years. It met on a monthly basis. Sometimes the members arrived feeling tired or burdened in some way which meant that the thought of presenting personal material and working on it with the group was not very attractive – it all felt too much effort. Likewise, the thought of getting involved in another member's problems felt like more work. Over the years the group had found a solution to meetings when this mood prevailed. It played a game called 'Let's discuss what this group is about'. During this game the members gave of themselves fully, repeating past positions, agonizing about roles and targets, talking generally about changing needs, and so on. Everybody could relax. On the surface the group was at work. However, the true objective was to avoid 'real' group work because few members felt like it at the time. The spurious work (it never really led to any significant changes) covered up true intentions while giving the appearance to all concerned of an industrious group hard at work. Obviously, this is similar to the group theme interpretation above. However, we would regard it to be a group game because it was re-enacted with some regularity, always with the same outcome and always with the same sense of relaxed relief.

In the terms of your post-group review you may thus find it helpful to ask the question, 'Did my group settle into pursuing a particular theme today and, if so, was that theme familiar from past meetings?' The element of repetition is a helpful guide in the attempt to identify group 'games'. *When a group regularly returns to a set of interactions that are played out like a predictable dance sequence, then suspect that there is an entrenched group 'game' involved.* The 'payoff' to the game may not be immediately obvious but a talk with your supervisor may help to shed some light on it.

Berne (1966) gives an insight into some of the 'games' which may be encountered. These will include 'psychiatry' – where the group accepts an offer from one or more of its members to wrestle interminably with insoluble personal problems. Later, the members may switch into a follow-up game called 'I'm only trying to help you'. In this, the group members, having become blocked and frustrated by their inevitable failure to impose a solution onto the 'patient', divest themselves of the responsibility of trying to help on the basis that it is impossible to help such people. In his various works, Berne (1964, 1966, 1972) describes many such 'games'. You may find it time well spent to go through some of his material.

Individual psychodynamics and the support group

Working with groups means that we have to accept that, fairly frequently, the apparent causes of a particular sequence of events or exchanges turn out not to be the reasons at all, but the result of other unrecognized influences operating on the group at a level below immediate consciousness. As a way of expanding this concept, we would like to introduce a further two theoretical concepts that can help to explain puzzling group events or developments between supervisor and supervisee (as described in the last chapter). These individual psychodynamic 'mechanisms' are: (1) transference and counter-transference; and (2) projection.

Transference and counter-transference
As adults we do not come absolutely fresh to any new situation, but carry with us memories of what happened to us on similar occasions in the past, and how we felt about them. Thus, if for instance a group member's last experience of a group situation was in school, no matter how long ago that was, how they felt about teachers and school then will permeate, perhaps dominate, their current feelings and attitude. Any such feelings may be said to be *transferred* from the past to the present but they will feel as if they belong to 'now'. It may be some time before the current experience cancels out the previous memories. In this scenario, the member may 'see' the leader as an authority figure, and act accordingly. This may be the case regardless of how the new leader is actually behaving and feeling.

The unwitting leader, meanwhile, may detect these sometimes hostile feelings, and react. Strangely, the old teacher–pupil relationship can be replayed as if it were currently valid. Obviously, if there were anything amiss in the old days, the present situation may be affected for the worse. What is more, this old struggle may be playing at an unconscious level in both parties. It may well be only after the skilled attention of a good supervisor that it becomes apparent to the leader that the member is not really, say, a provocative, cheeky adolescent, but a nervous adult. Furthermore, the leader also may be dismayed to realize how readily the role of punitive authority figure had been taken up. The leader may have found feelings stirring in response to those received from the member, i.e. *counter-transference* feelings, and have been mystified as to where these feelings came from, when in fact they constitute an excellent communication from the member about how she herself was feeling. In general, then, if a member of a group seems to be behaving in a way that suggests that they are 'getting it wrong' in relation to others in the group, it may be a case of transference making itself felt.

It should be recognized that these theoretical suggestions are possibilities, not absolute fact, and are relevant only if they are seen to be helpful. However, the concepts are widely accepted, and often provide a way forward. Furthermore, if you do not find the theories convincing, there is then a need to find some other, more convincing explanation for the phenomena that gave rise to the theories in the first place.

Projection

In March 2005 the BBC broadcast a series of programmes entitled *Blame the Parents*, billed as a 'group to improve parenting skills' (in which case the title was perhaps a little unfortunate). The statement was made that 'The priority at the first meeting is to help parents relax, that this is an OK place to be, with other people who will listen to them'. So far, so good, but then one of the parents, a lone mother, rushed out of a fairly early meeting of the group in tears, after accusing the leader of saying all kinds of things that, in fact, she had not said nor felt - to the visible distress of the leader, who had been steadily promoting sound strategies for managing difficult home situations. We, the viewers, had the advantage of seeing the struggle this mother had been having in trying to implement some of the improvements suggested within the group. She had found it very heavy going indeed, so much so that she had decided that the group must think badly of her and so be disapproving and overbearing. Bravely, she turned up at the next meeting, but full of anxious apprehension. In fact, the expected treatment was not handed out to her but such was the intensity of her own feeling that she acted *as if* her worst fears had been justified. She appeared to be unable to hear the group's reassurances and sympathy. It could be surmised that she had *projected* her own feelings onto the group. She couldn't bear it, and ran out, soon to be followed by a co-leader anxious to try and look after her. It was some time before she could bring herself to return, but she did eventually manage it after coming to terms with her own feelings of self-disapproval. In this example the unfortunate leader was having to cope with tumultuous emotions she could only guess at, both as they happened in the group and in the aftermath.

May we once again stress that all the above ideas are attempts by theorists to explain what may be happening in the group. They are relevant only inso far as you, the support group leader, find them to be applicable and useful in answering questions regarding outcomes of the group. They can usefully be discussed in supervision sessions.

Group patterns and the leader's intervention

We begin this section with a word of caution. There is a danger for the support group leader in so-called 'games analysis'. The leader risks being distracted by 'trying to spot the game'. That is, spending time in the group as a sort of suspicious detective, preoccupied with working out the group pattern in terms of 'games theory'. This, in itself, could be construed as a game since it has a ritualistic quality and leads to a clear pay-off – it allows the leader to feel superior. Support groups are not about 'games analysis'. Equally, support group leaders should not be functioning as group analysts. They should be present as gentle facilitators, maintaining a warm, human presence. This is difficult if the leader is set apart from the group offering the occasional, challenging interpretation.

It is essential to remember that your job as group leader is to help the group achieve its objectives. *Therefore, the kind of concepts we have been discussing will be called into use only if you judge that the group is 'disabled'.* By this we mean seriously off target because it has become dominated by activity that fits the pattern of a non-productive group solution to a threat, or is given over to some form of Berne-style 'game'. You do not have to be absolutely certain that this is the case, but if you have got to the point of feeling worried that something is wrong, then it is reasonable enough to act. The action, as always, is simply to share your thoughts and feelings with the group in an easy, non-threatening manner, thereby encouraging them to examine their true motives in engaging in their current activity. For example, the leader of the support group who regularly avoided work by ruminations on the group's real function might have made the following intervention:

> I'd just like to make a comment at this point, before we get into talking about the point of the group once more. We do this is a lot. I have been wondering if it is easier for us to be very rational and talk in these terms than to work on personal issues, especially if most of us are tired from lots of casework. I'm saying that our regular conversations on the point of the group might be a way of avoiding something. Will you pause a moment and make contact with your feelings and check if there is any truth in this?

Other considerations of patterns within a support group

Earlier in this chapter mention was made of the possibility that some members might take on semi-permanent roles within the group. Again it has to be stressed that this will not usually be a ploy which has been thought out, most likely the people involved will not have a well-developed awareness of the pattern. Such things may come and go in the group. You do not necessarily have to do anything about it unless you feel that it is hindering the group in its pursuit of agreed objectives, or that some useful learning might be achieved if you were to point out what was happening. The development of the roles may be insidious with a member tentatively offering a style of contribution in the group and this becoming 'locked in' because it suited the needs of the group at the time. For example:

- *The group initiator* – this member takes on the responsibility to get things moving and break silences.
- *The group jester* – a member who defuses tension or keeps the atmosphere safely trivial.
- *The group patient(s)* – one or more members who can be relied upon to present problems, often of an ongoing nature, thus providing convenient content for a group on many occasions.
- *The group parents* – members who respond to those relating in a 'child-state' (see Berne (1964)) by offering a reassuring, advice-giving, parent-like pattern of responses.
- *The group challenger* – a member who takes on the responsibility to express discontent with the group and challenge the leader over specific issues or even for temporary leadership.
- *The group recluse* – a member who attracts attention by persisting in a withdrawn, non-participating manner.
- *The group harmonizer* – a member who acts to defuse any tension or expressions of anger.
- *The group mystery person* – a member who takes part in much of the group discussion but manages to avoid presenting personal material. Quite often someone in this role will also communicate that there is much material to present but that it cannot be done 'here or now'.

Finally, it is important to remember the obvious but important fact that people attend a group within a personal, domestic and work context. They may, therefore, bring into the group their 'emotional luggage' but might be unaware of so doing. That is, their style of relating in the group will reflect their feelings from the broader context of their life just as described above in the section dealing with transference.

Taking a broad view, this chapter has been about sensitizing you to some of the influences which may direct your group for a while. Such things affect all groups and are part of 'people getting on together'. You need only intervene when it is clear to you that the group is neither progressing nor profiting from the time spent together because it is set into a distracting group defence, or diverted by a member assuming a particular role. Thus you should be able to ask 'What is the group engaged upon at this moment and what is this business about?' You cannot order the group to change its ways. However, most members are able to engage in the adult-to-adult style of interacting which we look for in a group and work on their important issues if the opportunity presents itself. Therefore, if you take the initiative to share your thoughts and observations with the group, this may be all that is needed to enable them to understand what has been happening and shift into more productive work. For instance, a leader might try saying:

> During the last half hour I have noticed that Jack has kept us all light-hearted with his jokes and we have all joined in. I just need to check that this is how you want to spend the time today and that we are not using Jack's humour as a way of avoiding something less pleasant.

Further reading on these general themes can be found in Dryden and Thorne (1991), especially in the chapter by Shohet and Wilmot and also the chapter by Hawkins and Shohet. Finlay (1993) covers useful ground in her chapter entitled 'Managing problems in a group'.

7　Ending a support group

The lifespans of different types of support group will vary enormously. At one end of the scale, some short-term groups will operate on a contract, specifying as few as five meetings. In contrast, long-term groups may have no agreed life and, if successful, may run for years. One group, to our knowledge, a support group for counsellors, is still running after 25 years, with many of the original members still attending. In this case, the members regard attendance at the group as part of their work and professional duty. Hence there is a work-related justification for such longevity. Much the same will apply to many staff support groups.

At one time or another, though, every group must draw to a close and thus the members must deal with the severance of group support. In these terms we believe that it is important to pay just as much attention to the process of finishing, letting go and moving on, as it is to any other phase of group life. As always, groups offer opportunities for learning. Taking part in the ending of a group presents an excellent chance for the members to explore, experience and learn how to cope with departures and the loss of support figures in a constructive way. At the same time, old feelings of sadness and loss that may be related to half-resolved personal losses from earlier in life can 'surface' (the issue of transference again). The ending process gives an opportunity to rework these past losses and gain some mastery over the problem. Overall, this process does not have to be a gloomy business. The parting, even with regrets, can signal the start of a new phase in life, which can be undertaken optimistically in the knowledge that the group members are a little better equipped and a little stronger to deal with the demands upon them.

Constructing an ending

In many ways, the tasks facing the support group leader are similar to those of ending a one-to-one counselling relationship. Marx and Gelso (1987) described these tasks as being 'reviewing the counselling, thinking about the future, and saying good-bye'. For some group members, the group leader and certain other members may have become very significant people – sometimes taking on a feel of 'family'. Members may have found the cohesion and safe environment for discussing feelings quite unique. The thought of doing without these can be alarming and such feelings may well provoke group dynamics in the manner discussed above. The ending of the group, the experiences had in the group, the personal effect of the group on members and the strategies for coping without the group have to be discussed openly for the feelings to be resolved and to give the members the opportunity to prepare for being without the group.

We can follow this process at work in the final meeting in a support group that had been set up for community workers. The ending of the group meetings had been clearly established in advance, scheduled to be at the completion of 20 meetings. As part of the process of disbandment, the leader invited the group to discover what had happened to each member during these 20 meetings. The aim of this was to give members the chance to get things in perspective and to remind themselves just how things had been for them at the beginning. Once that had been done, then to remember how it had been along the way and, finally, to notice and share how they were feeling and thinking as the group closed. They would then be able to say their goodbyes appropriately, and turn their thoughts to the future. To assist in this task the leader was directive at this point and invited the members to sit quietly for a while and try to recapture the way they had felt when first coming to the group. When they felt ready, they were to talk to one other member and listen carefully to what the other had to say, and then recount their own experience. Finally, if they wished, they could share anything they wanted to with the whole group. We reproduce some of the responses below.

'What I came with'

> I came reluctant to start, not valuing myself, not wanting to make any commitment. I had difficulty in sharing my feelings.
>
> (Carol)

> I felt very unsure. I thought the others would all be more experienced and cleverer than me. I was very self-critical, and thought of myself as a good listener but a failed person.
>
> (Margaret)

> I was angry at the start. I had a fear of opening the box again. But it wasn't so bad. The group turned out to be a good place to do it.
>
> (Marilyn)

> I felt estranged from the world at large at the end of a 30 year relationship.
>
> (Esther)

> Anxious, thinking it was self-indulgent to take up the time of others.
>
> (David)

It can be seen that these people came with a wide range of concerns and emotions, many of them negative. Given the opportunity by the leaders, they were able to register with great clarity how their life had been, what they had brought with them to the group, and to share their perceptions of themselves. By doing so, a benchmark was established against which they could recognize, measure and acknowledge any gains subsequently made. It is worth noting that the members would have been too blocked by their fears and anxieties to share their feelings if they had been asked to talk about themselves right at the beginning.

'Along the way'

After reflecting on the time the group had spent together in the past, members reported their memories of how they had experienced the group. Our same members had this to say, among other things:

> I felt myself exploring new ways of being with people and gaining in confidence. I felt pain and fear, and learned that it is OK to be where you are, and progress.
>
> (Carol)

> I came across my own not-nice stuff, but that was OK, I still had something to offer.
>
> (Margaret)

> I've really appreciated the personal support since my mother died. And for the first time I've really felt the power of a professional support group as well. There's no-one else who really listens. (Marilyn's mother had died in the time the group had been meeting.)
>
> (Marilyn)

Other quotes:

> I was surprised at others' concern when I cried and I've personally dealt with a strong difficulty with receiving negative feedback.
>
> (Esther)

> I've found the confidence to act and initiate in a group and I've suddenly started using skills outside the group.
>
> (David)

These first-hand quotations capture in a most vivid way how life in a support group can be, what discoveries can be made along the way. The purpose of giving time for reflection as the group was drawing to a close was to allow the members time to crystallize their experience, catch hold of it while the memories were fresh, and lodge the worthwhile parts in their long-term memory.

'Here and now'

Finally, the members turned their attention to the present, and began to think about their future plans. Thus:

> I really need to consolidate now, both my head and my feelings, make a new commitment.
>
> (Carol)

> I'm now much more self-accepting than ever before. It's OK for me to speak, or not to speak, as I wish, to find my own level. I'm nervous at going forward, but I can handle it now.
>
> (Margaret)

> I give more in my personal life. I can see a big rift between my two selves, and the way I perceive my working conditions. In some ways I feel deskilled, but I can see how it could be better, how to improve. We've learned how to use and support each other; I personally have learned to be at ease sometimes and not always hurrying on. (Marilyn was making a distinction between her super-efficient, busy, high-achieving, organizing self, and her more emotional, feeling self, both part of her personality.)
>
> (Marilyn)

> It feels so different now. I've gained self-confidence and strength from the group. I'm more light-hearted in every aspect of my life.
>
> (Esther)

> I've learned it's OK to be me, that I'm entitled to a fulfilling life too.
>
> (David)

The leader's invitation to review the experience of the group made it easier to chart the changes that had occurred. Members were able to secure their own individual learning, describe their gains coherently, and take satisfaction in their progress. The leader and the group found this a very moving session, where quite personal material was being openly shared and received. The review served to 'clear the decks' so that members could begin to envisage how life would be without the group. The final questions the group discussed were 'Where do we go from here? What are our plans for the future?'

Figure 23 Goodbye

Goodbye

It is time now to put your faith in the group's ability to cope, and allow members to handle their goodbyes as they see fit. Your job as leader is simply to make sure that enough time is available, that everyone understands when 'just before the end' is, so that no-one is forced to leave things unsaid from lack of time' (Cox 1978).

There are many strategies available to you as group leader, but we feel it is as well to go for the genuineness of the moment, with a proviso that it is a good idea to look for positive messages that people can take away and cherish. It is no bad thing for you as leader to open up a little more than is usual, in order to deliver your own messages to the group. For instance, if you are pleased with the progress made, there's no harm in saying so. It is a good time to confront people with their strengths, and to encourage them to remind each other what to remember, and take away. Fragments overheard in one closing session included: 'Don't put yourself down, or discount your own feelings.' 'Be direct, don't flinch, communicate.' 'Look after yourself. Your emotions aren't lethal if they're attended to.'

At the very end, people will make their goodbyes in different ways, but do not be surprised if members become very emotional. It is by no means un-usual to find that even groups that have been comparatively reserved can dissolve into tears and hugs before finally disbanding. Others may settle for a quiet goodbye, or repairing to the pub. The important thing is that, as leader, you stay watchful and caring as ever. It is a good plan to make sure that you are the last to leave, or at least stay around quietly available until you're sure that anyone who wants to talk to you has had ample opportunity to do so. Finally, do not forget to attend to your own feelings at the end of the group, and to your own goodbyes.

Resistance to ending the group

We recommended in Chapter 5 that some thought be given at the beginning to making an explicit contract as to the number of meetings and their duration, the terms of which were clear to all. Such early care pays off as the sequence draws to a close, as everyone knows when the ending will be, and can pace themselves accordingly.

You may notice that nevertheless there may be some resistance to the group's dissolution. Strong pleas may be heard for more meetings, and arrangements for reunions may be in the wind. We would not wish to disparage any such moves, as some group members may well stay in touch beneficially long after the group has ceased. Indeed, one regional counselling association had its origins in just such a way. However, we do think considerable caution needs to be exercised by the leader, and further plans should be considered carefully. There often seems to be much ambivalence in the members, insofar as they wish at one level to continue the contract, but at another to be free of it, to develop new and satisfying relationships in the outside world. If the group originally contracted to finish after, say, ten sessions, then maybe it should finish when session ten comes along.

Loss

Part of the ambivalence we describe can come from an unwillingness to face the impending loss of the group, and the support that it gives. The loss will be real enough, although hopefully group members will have reached a point where they can successfully provide a substitute, as was evident with the community workers group described earlier. If further support is needed, part of the closing meeting can be used to help members to locate and utilize their own resources, perhaps friends, colleagues or family. As with any loss, it is important to give people time to come to terms with it, to talk about it, and cry if they need to.

If this should seem in any way exaggerated, it is as well to remember that memories of previous partings, perhaps even of the loss of close relations, can be triggered by the approaching loss of the group. For instance, at the end of a weekend-long group, one of the participants suddenly said, 'I thought I was all right, but I find myself thinking about my father's death', a memory that had been submerged for quite a while. Clearly, a caring leader, and group, will want and need to give space and attention at such times. Now, it may seem somewhat brutal, but the leader's job just then may also be to remind the group of how much (or how little) time is left for personal work, that even though someone is on the brink of deeply emotional material, we soon have to end. It may be necessary, after giving time to acknowledge the emotion, and the power of the memory, nevertheless to make sure that the person puts away the experience for the time being, comes back to the present, and makes ready to go home.

It is important too, in the drama of negotiating last-minute powerful material, that all the available time and attention do not get used up on the one member, important though they are, but that somehow space is found for everyone else. After all, a nervous person may be keeping equally stirring things inside themselves, not wishing to impose, and go away upset, and unsatisfied. As leader, it's necessary to try and keep some balance in proceedings and, as ever, ensure that everyone gets the chance to say what they need to say.

So far we have been discussing the straightforward circumstance when all members finish at the same time, by agreement and in good order. Many support groups, however, run on a different basis, over a long period. Individuals will leave over time, and new members join. Such changes can be accommodated, so long as it's been agreed as a policy (see our earlier discussion on open groups), but will still need a high degree of care and alertness on the part of the leader. Very similar processes to those described for the whole group will be at work when an individual leaves while the group continues.

For a person to leave in good order, and leaving no restlessness in the remaining group, the leader needs to manage things so that ample time is devoted to the emotions of the person departing, and of those remaining. At one level or another, partings arouse much feeling. The process of loss is often accompanied by a kind of mourning. No matter how glad the group may be for the person leaving – perhaps to a new job, or a new life – their going will still be registered as a loss. At a subconscious level, there are sometimes unreasonable angry feelings around, perhaps at the leaver, for leaving or getting better, perhaps at the leader for not preventing it, or even at life generally for dealing out yet another loss.

Occasionally, the leaver may, for his or her own reasons, be bent on leaving the group in some disorder, maybe departing as a result of their own problems and limitations. Clues that this might be happening can be:

- A 'scene' is precipitated, with feeling running high, ending in a dramatic exit apparently 'caused' by mishandling by the leader, the group, or selected individuals within the group. (Note that this is different from the case where a member really has been abused by the group, or an incompetent or off-form leader, and has retired in sheer self-defence.)

- A member simply disappears, just not turning up, and offering no explanation nor apology. They may well have been taking a prominent part in business until then.
- A member fails to arrive, as above, but somehow manages to filter often contradictory messages by circuitous routes into the group.
- A member may speak privately to the leader, explaining why they are departing, sometimes exonerating the leader, but deliver a quite different message to the group, or part of it.

At all events, the leader will notice a bewilderment, dismay, disarray and general upset in the group, which will require attention. It might be sufficient to point out that the group seems to be spending more time on the absent member(s) than on those present. It may well be difficult to secure a clean closure in the face of such messy departures, and the group may just have to wrestle with the issues. The leader's task is to encourage the group to move on through distress and back on to more productive, on-target issues. If the group is permitted to worry unchallenged about the harm it fears has been done, it may actually fall into such chaos and disrepair that the meetings are abandoned; not a desirable outcome.

We should return now to more positive aspects of endings and give a summary of points to bear in mind.

- Sooner or later people may need to move on from their group and this can be managed well or badly.
- There may well be ambivalence around the ending of a group, or an individual's leaving it, which may lead to contradictory currents in the group.
- Just before the end is a good time to review the gains achieved by the group.
- It is necessary to pay attention to feelings of loss, to talk them over, and register the loss. This is the time to choose how to remember the group, its members, the experiences that the members have had within it.
- This is a good time to establish optimism and hope by considering future plans. What are members going to do next, and how are they going to sustain their progress?
- Time is needed in which to make proper goodbyes.

Self-help groups

One device for continuing the life of a group is conversion into a self-help format. Self-help groups, as the name suggests, function without a formal leader. Clearly there can be difficulties to be faced in making this move since the loss of the leader can seem catastrophic. However, where resources are limited yet clients or staff still need support, it may be the only viable option. Lakin (1985) devotes a section of his text to this type of group and other than mentioning the option we will not discuss them further.

8   Supervision and evaluation
The support and development of the group leader

> The role of listeners has never been fully appreciated. However, it is well known that most people don't listen. They use the time when someone else is speaking to think of what they're going to say next. True listeners have always been revered among oral cultures, and prized for their rarity value; bards and poets are ten a cow, but a good listener is hard to find, or at least hard to find twice.
>
> (Pratchett 1989)

Up to this point, we have considered the support group mainly from the perspective of what is most helpful to the members. It's now time to think more of the specific needs of the group leader in terms of support and supervision.

Why does a support group leader need support?

Throughout this book we have sought to maintain an air of encouragement to those thinking of establishing a support group of their own. However, we acknowledge that there are difficulties in working with groups in a supportive capacity. Even the most eminent and experienced therapists encounter personal dilemmas both during and as a result of their work. A sensitive discussion of some of these issues can be found in Dryden (1985). Indeed, the need for some kind of consultative support for such workers has become so widely recognized that many in the helping professions are required to have regular recourse to skilled and reliable colleagues in a supervisory capacity in order to establish and maintain their accreditation as competent professionals (e.g. see the requirements of the British Association for Counselling and Psychotherapy for members seeking professional accreditation, as described in the Ethical Framework for Good Practice in Counselling and Psychotherapy (2002). *We strongly recommend that support group leaders of whatever degree of experience similarly find someone with whom they can safely discuss their group work, and examine their thoughts and feelings on the progress of their group, its members, and especially how these are affecting the leader.* Such work is often called 'supervision', a somewhat misleading term, as it is often used in the workplace to mean the ensuring of a satisfactory quality of work done by a junior, less experienced worker by a senior, responsible overseer, and has overtones of authoritarian intervention. While there are some elements of this kind of relationship, we have in mind a much more supportive setting within which a group leader can feel safe, free to explore any difficulties or successes they might encounter, without fear of being made to feel inept by ridicule or reproach. Such a process is better described as 'consultant supervision' but perhaps the actual term is unimportant so long as the participants seek and find a productive working relationship.

What is consultant supervision?

Consultant supervision is a process whereby the actual practice of a support group leader is examined closely by that leader, working with the assistance of an experienced colleague. Between them, it should be possible for the leader to identify strengths, where what was done had proved effective and helpful, and other times when the contributions were not so successful, possibly even hindering the group in its work. Once identified, it should be possible to work together to reinforce the strengths and improve on any weaknesses. The content and the process of a supervision session will depend on the nature of the contract established at the outset (see below). The activity is designed to promote the following:

1   the support and protection of the leader;
2   the furtherance of leader skills, awareness, and technique;
3   the protection of the group members.

Why is consultant supervision important?

The point of such work is to ensure that the members consistently receive the best the leader can offer, so that the group experience is productive, fulfilling, and satisfying for members and leader(s) alike. The second pair of eyes is to ensure that the leader doesn't overlook clues in feelings and behaviours that can point to 'blind spots', perhaps fixed ideas, or prejudice. Such clues may be apparent to an objective observer, but elude a leader caught up in the moment – sometimes one 'can't see the wood for the trees'. In raising what may seem to be obvious issues with the leader, habits of thought and other internal psychological processes can be brought into conscious awareness, and thus made available for discussion and perhaps modification. This is not to imply for one moment that new group leaders are full of prejudice. It is more that prejudice is often blatantly clear when some *other* person is holding a

Figure 24 The process of consultant supervision

prejudice, such as 'all men are insensitive', or 'most doctors are out of touch with their patients', and so on. However, *our own* prejudices are not so easy to spot, and we may not even know we have them until they make an appearance in some aspect of our group work.

Case study Becoming an expert

A number of practitioners had come together with a view to their becoming supervisors. An external facilitator was engaged to help the group to focus on their objective. At one juncture, one of the members had been describing a session where she had expertise in the area in which her client had been experiencing difficulty. The facilitator commented on this by way of reflection to the effect that she appeared to have offered expert assistance. He was somewhat taken aback when this ostensibly innocuous contribution prompted a furious reaction in the original presenter, and he had to work hard to stay calm in the face of angry tears and energetic verbal attack. After a while, when things had calmed down a little, it transpired that the presenter had suffered greatly in the past at the hands of 'experts', so much so that to imply she herself enjoyed 'expert' status was an outrageous insult to her – she was in fact heavily prejudiced against 'experts', but had not been conscious of this. As it happened, to the members of this particular group it was vital that if they were to become useful supervisors to other practitioners they needed to become comfortable with recognizing and owning their own expertise, which on occasion might indeed be very useful to their potential supervisees, some of whom might well be inexperienced.

By the very nature of the role, the leader will be looked to for the proper handling of the group's business. As described earlier, pre-group decisions about appropriate ground rules for the start will have had to be made and explained, and there will be a continuous stream of further decisions to be made as the group unfolds. These will include matters of timing, negotiating starting and stopping, how much time can be devoted to a particular member or topic, when to try and move on, and crucially if, when, and how to intervene. There will be decisions regarding leadership style – 'Shall I try and involve the whole group in all decisions? How far can I direct matters without appearing to be too autocratic and self-centred? Should I be trying to "do" anything anyway?' and so on. It can readily be seen that these are all decisions the leader will have to take regarding leader behaviour, in relation to how the group is itself behaving. There are likely to be questions that leave a leader wondering about his or her own behaviour: 'I wonder why I was so bossy in the group today? What was it that affected me so much that I can't put it out of my mind even now when I'm sitting quietly at home trying to relax? They seemed unusually sulky today, was that anything to do with me, is it my fault? What should I have noticed that I didn't?' – the possibilities are endless.

Case study 'What do I do next?'

A well-established support group of counsellors seemed to be having trouble settling to their business, which was to focus on how their therapeutic work was going and, in particular, how it was affecting them personally. There was much desultory conversation, about the traffic, weather, the shortcomings of other services and personnel. As an experienced professional group, their group contract included individual responsibility for claiming group time, and for the proper use of that time. Be that as it may, after a little while, the leader, having noticed this change in routine, decided to bring the apparent reluctance to the group's attention. The response was split. While some of the group were apparently surprised at the observation, as they had themselves 'not noticed', others in the group said more or less that they had indeed noticed, and wondered what it was about. Even so, they had not voiced their feeling, and were going along with the rest of the group, apparently unable or unwilling to do anything about it. Clearly this was a telling decision for the leader, who was then left with a further question – 'What do I do next, for the best?' Such a sequence can be very puzzling for both leader and members, and there may be little time to resolve such difficulties as they occur in the group, where events sometimes come thick and fast – it is very easy to feel one step (or more) behind as things unfold, on occasions with great speed, leaving the leader with much to think about and puzzle over after the group, including, 'Was that the best I could do? Should I change anything next time? I wonder why I'm feeling like this – how am I feeling anyway?', and so on.

It is not only behaviour that can engage the leader's thoughts, but the actual content of the words spoken. Every member will have their own story to tell, and some of the details can be very moving indeed. Histories of abuse of all kinds, physical, emotional, sexual, bullying at work suffered by members young or old, are likely to be present in a group set up specifically for support. Sometimes people have suffered from overwhelming life events, which may well touch on the leader's own personal history, and be very difficult to accommodate in the flow of the group. Does a leader choose to share, or not share, their own details with the group members? If so, how much, and when – after all, the group is not there primarily for the benefit of the leader? If not, how to explain the leader's own personal reaction in the group when deeply affected by the emotions in the group, for the members are likely to notice either way. A leader's functionality can be considerably affected for the worse unless some way can be found to accommodate emotions aroused within the group, and by the group.

Case example Handling strong emotions

A counsellor in a GP practice noticed that the doctors had referred a small but very distinct number of patients, all of whom were in need of her care as a result of their being bereaved by the loss of a child. She conceived the idea of setting up a support group for them, to help them in the task of experiencing their grief, then picking up their lives again in the face of devastating loss. She introduced the idea to each potential group member individually with great care and caution, discussing how it might be for them, what possible advantages and difficulties they might find there, paying appropriate attention to what we described in Chapter 4 as 'pre-group preparation'. She was heartened to find that in general the idea was well received, and the group was duly set up. It was very effective, succeeding in its aims. What the counsellor had difficulty negotiating, however, was not the tears and pain, which she expected and for which she was prepared, but that she felt deeply moved by the positive qualities of resilience and care for others in the group shown by the members, and her own feelings of inadequacy in the face of their strength, having suffered so much. She subsequently found it very helpful when she was able to explore these feelings with her own consultant/ supervisor after the group, and resolve them sufficiently to enable her work to progress, recognizing that although she had felt insufficiently skilled in these circumstances, in fact she had handled the strong emotions in the group really very well.

Thus, through these examples, we hope that we have shown that a support group leader who has the resource of a consultant supervisor has an advantage. To take issues arising from the support group to a supervision session and there to reflect on the strategy that the leader has adopted provides the leader with support and companionship, together with a situation that allows for insight and learning.

Finding a supervisor – what should be sought and requested?

In the preceding paragraphs we have already given strong hints as to what kind of response in a consultant/supervisor could be useful to a leader. Of course, the choice of such a resource will be a highly personal one, as the relationship will demand utter trust in both parties. It might be helpful, however, to consider how other professionals in the field think about their needs. In 2004 we conducted an informal survey of a number of very experienced, professionally qualified therapists and group workers in the South-West of England, who were willing to share their personal thoughts about their own needs and choices concerning the ideal supervisor. They were asked, 'What do you need in a supervisor and the supervision session?'

The qualities looked for were not too dissimilar from those which equip people to be competent and efficient personal therapists. Within the counselling profession it is commonly held that a competent practitioner will possess at least three core abilities, namely:

1   The capacity and willingness to be able to accept whatever is being said to them without rushing to judge and parade their own opinions, an aspect usually termed *acceptance*. An alternative term is 'unconditional (or non-judgmental) positive regard', by means of which a positive attitude towards a person is maintained no matter what.

2   Being able to see the world as far as possible through the eyes and experience of their client, to feel 'where their shoes pinch', almost as if the same things were happening to the counsellors themselves, but without ever losing the awareness that they are not. This is usually termed *empathic understanding*, and requires considerable concentration, intellect, and imagination.

3   The ability to be open and honest in their own speech and behaviour, so that there are no mixed messages, hidden agendas, or misleading behavioural cues. This is often termed *congruence*. To be effective, such behaviour must not be in any way simulated, but needs to have been absorbed into the practitioner's usual approach to the world – to be congruent or sincere is not something you do to people, it is something you are or are not.

It may be seen that there is some contradiction between (1) and (3), but in practice counsellors and clientele usually manage to work out a satisfactory functioning relationship, and so do supervisors and supervisees.

Our own small sample of various different practitioners confirmed that they would all be looking for similar qualities as a prerequisite in their own consultant supervisors. Thus, a response from a front-line worker in a drugs counselling agency showed a requirement in his supervisor and supervision sessions for: 'Honesty; an ability to listen and reflect; able to help me see the wider picture; able to help me recognize my own strengths, weaknesses and vulnerabilities; able to recognize and focus on my actual roles at work. And a comfortable chair.'

Similarly, a widely known, veteran therapist, very senior in a national professional counselling organization, says: 'I need a supervisor who does not intrude but who gives time and space for me to reflect on the process. But [who] can also make me uncomfortably aware that I have not been as professional as I would like.' This latter comment introduces an element of challenge, and a concern for the maintenance of a professional level of delivery of service – there is a wider responsibility to other professionals in the field, and towards the public at large. Thus, an experienced alcohol counsellor looks for someone who is 'warm and understanding, but won't take any bulls**t'.

The strength of the supervisee–supervisor relationship is likely to be developed by a process of honest acknowledgment and subsequent exploration in a non-judgmental atmosphere of anything causing concern – mistakes, misunderstandings, blind spots, and so on. No matter how experienced and skilful we might be, we all make mistakes sooner or later; indeed, for learning to take place, it might actually be necessary that mistakes should be made. The best plan is to seek to limit their effects, recognize, acknowledge and 'own them' early on. The most important thing is to learn from them, and move on, apologizing if necessary, but without making too much unwarranted fuss. *The focus needs to be on rewarding useful and constructive actions and responses,* thus reinforcing good practice, rather than on fault-finding. It might even be necessary for a supervisor to encourage a new leader not to be overly self-critical, and not waste time on recriminations, but to be properly attentive to where improvements need to be made and change things for the better.

It can be taken as read that it is preferable for the consultant/supervisor to have had some first-hand personal experience of the kind of work being undertaken, so that two minds can focus solely on any difficulties that the group leader is encountering. It's not really sufficient to be a well-meaning good friend, and unless a spouse or partner is experienced in their own right, there are many difficulties in the way of using such people as a means of providing supportive and productive discussion. At the same time, we recognize that properly experienced and qualified supervisors can be very hard to find, and may well be expensive. In the counselling profession a number of training courses for supervisors have been established, and a system for the formal accreditation of recognized supervisors has been inaugurated. Names of accredited counselling supervisors are available from BACP. Even so, these are comparatively early days in the professional development of supervision, and provision can be patchy. There is a continuing debate as to the most suitable format, and a number of different approaches are being explored, as discussed by Lawton (2000). If for whatever reason, proper consultation is not available, we believe it is still better to talk things over with a non-advice-giving trusted friend or colleague than to battle on absolutely alone. To be safe and effective, however, any such a person must be able to respect your confidence and not gossip, and not leap too quickly to their own conclusions and advice. We owe ourselves a professional duty of self-care, in order to maintain our own effectiveness, and to safeguard our own health. Our reference to the 'Care Trap' in Chapter 1 needs to be kept in mind – hard-pressed group leaders are by no means immune. Readers wishing to enquire further can find a very useful survey of counselling supervision issues in Dryden and Thorne (1991).

The basic ingredients of a supervision session

As an introduction to what might happen in a supervision session, perhaps we might listen in to an exchange between Linda, an experienced leader, and Helen, a colleague who is venturing into running her first group, and is a bit anxious about how she'll find it:

> *Helen*: Linda, thanks for taking the time to talk to me about this group of mine. I'm quite looking forward to it, but I'm a bit nervous, too.
>
> *Linda*: That doesn't surprise me, as I can still remember how I was before my first group, and it brings it all back to me. How would you like me to help?
>
> *Helen*: I'm not too sure just yet, but it would be good to think I could come and compare notes afterwards, and maybe get a few tips and hints about anything that's bothering me.
>
> *Linda*: OK, I'll be happy to discuss things with you, but with the understanding that this is your group, and will be different from mine. I'll concentrate on trying to understand how it feels to be you in the group, what you find happening from your point of view, rather than mine or even the group's. It's very unlikely I'll be able to tell you what to do, and you might not thank me for it if I did, but if you feel you could've done something a bit differently we could think it through together and see what you come up with. How's that?
>
> *Helen*: That sounds good to me. Can we sort out a time to do it? And while

we're at it, I need to know if you would like me to pay you for your time and experience. I would like that to be clear, so I know it's OK for me to call on you.

Linda: I appreciate your saying that, but I'm happy to do this in normal working hours. Part of my job is Staff Development. I've discussed it with my boss, and she thinks it's a really good idea. When would you like to make a start?

When the first supervision session takes place, what can Helen reasonably expect to have happen? This will depend to a very large extent on what concerns she is bringing, so Linda's first task will be *to listen most carefully to what is communicated*. She will need to pay special attention to how Helen is feeling as she introduces her agenda, paying attention not only to her words, but the manner in which she says them, and whatever other messages may be being conveyed. For instance, Helen may be 'upbeat' and encouraged by the way her group went, and so be light in tone. Or if things had not gone so well, there might well be a leaden feeling to her words as she recalls the experience, a sigh or two (of which she may be totally unaware). She may find herself pacing the room, or conversely sitting passive, waiting to be 'told things'. Whatever she introduces, she can expect it to be picked up and gently reflected by Linda, and taken seriously, no matter how trivial Helen feels it to be, along with an invitation to explore a little more, to see if anything significant is interfering with Helen's conduct of her group. At the same time, it would be useful for Linda to keep careful track of her own feelings – on occasion, she too may find herself inexplicably smiling, or frowning, feeling anxious, sad, angry, and so on, without there being any immediately identifiable reason for such feelings. In such circumstances it is worth considering whether or not the feelings are some kind of communication at another level from Helen, or even from her group (see our earlier comments on transference and projection in Chapter 6).

> **Case study Re-thinking a valuation system**
> As an example of how this process might work in practice, a leader was running two adult groups of a similar nature, with different personnel, and on different days. She had a long-standing relationship with an experienced and trusted supervisor. During one session she ventured the opinion that group A was 'better' than group B, and consequently she didn't like being with group B as much. This was picked up by the supervisor, and together they had a closer look at what was going on here – the prime reason for the groups' existence was the same and they were not there primarily to give the leader enjoyment, nor to indulge her likes and dislikes. In fact, both groups were going about their business as best they knew how. A key question asked by the supervisor was, 'I wonder why you feel it

necessary to rank them in this way, how does it help the group's purpose? Have you any ideas why you find yourself doing it?' It transpired that the leader had been a teacher for much of her working life, and had acquired the habit of classifying, and making lists of 'merit', designating 'good' children and 'bad', resulting (as in much of the education system) in different treatment being given to the children according to their status. She was chastened to see how this habit had transferred from her former situation to this one, and might even be exacerbating the differences she thought she had detected. It was vital that no hint be given to group B that they were in any way inferior to the other group, as their already shaky morale could have been badly affected by such a view. The best way of ensuring this did not happen was for the leader to explore her feelings, hopefully re-think her valuation system and concentrate on the job in hand. Just as it is important not to have 'favourite' members in the group, for all need to be treated alike without fear or favour, so it was important that the groups be treated similarly. As a footnote, in time, group B did indeed settle down to their business just as effectively as group A – there never really had been that much difference between them in the first place. Note that it was absolutely right that the leader had been able to bring this issue to supervision, and was able to modify her approach as a result.

Preparation for supervision

By now you may well be thinking, 'Alright, I see the point and I've got my consultant lined up, but what should I be telling my supervisor about? It's important I don't waste our time and talk about the weather.' The reality is that if you have been fortunate enough to find yourself a really good listener, the time will fly past and you'll find it all too short. You may surprise yourself with just how much you have to say, and what feeling you find running inside yourself, and perhaps between you and the supervisor. It's probably a good idea to think in advance of what you would like to talk about, and do a re-run of the support group session in your mind. *A good plan would be to do this very soon after the group is over,* and again just before you see your consultant. Leaders often find it useful to *keep a log* after group session, in which significant items are recorded for later reflection. One practical framework is to consider what happened in the group from three separate perspectives:

1 *Behaviour* – who did what, when, how, and why?
2 *Thinking* – what ideas were around, what was the content of what was said?
3 *Feelings* – what emotion was prevalent in the group, and when? Did it change at all? In what way?

Completing such a task may seem onerous and tedious after a hard session, but if undertaken properly can provide an excellent source of evidence on which to ruminate and draw conclusions. The very effort of struggling to recall itself constitutes training, and becomes easier over time. Early attempts may be discouraging, in as much as it's often very difficult to remember what happened and when, let alone the feelings and thoughts that went with the events; but it becomes easier. Writing up the log gives at least some time in which to converse with oneself about how the group is going. Such internal conversation is a first step to developing skills as a leader, constituting as it does a private forum in which to review one's successes and mistakes alike, in order to improve and keep the group and oneself in good working order.

For good measure, here's another three headings to consider – try writing first in the first person, as in 'What did *I* do, think, feel?', etc. Then try the third person, i.e. 'What did *they* do, think, feel?', etc., and finally try the plural, 'What did *we* do, think, feel?', etc. One way or another, you'll probably generate enough material to be going on with and you will find you have plenty to talk about when you meet your supervisor. As you work together, you are likely to notice aspects of the group that puzzle you and merit further attention on your part. As a general guide, anything you find yourself thinking about after the group, perhaps days after, is appropriate to take to supervision, no matter how trivial it may seem, as are any feelings you may register, positive (elation, affection, pride in the group, etc.), or negative (disheartened, fed up, inadequate, unskilled, etc.). It is appropriate to consider them carefully, because often there is more going on in a group than meets the eye at first glance. Fairly frequently, apparent causes of a particular sequence of events or exchange turn out not to be the reasons at all, but the result of other unspoken or unrecognized influences operating on the group at a level below immediate consciousness.

Once you have done your pre-consultation preparation, it is often a good plan to set aside your carefully prepared written notes, and focus simply on whatever issues and feelings come up when you sit down with your supervisor. You may well be surprised at what you find yourself talking about; the connections with your group, its work, and your conscious concerns, may at first be elusive, but may become clearer as your session progresses. It's not unusual for a supervisee to say, 'Hmm. I didn't know I was going to talk about that', having unearthed some previously hidden aspect of their relationship with their group.

Supervision and personal therapy

The focus of consultant supervision is the professional relationship between leader and group. Both ends of that relationship have their own tangle of behaviour, thoughts, feelings and fantasies, and it is appropriate to look at them insofar as they impinge on the group and affect group business. 'The relationship' does not exist as a separate entity, but as the outcome of the interaction between the participants. In considering the leader's contribution to the relationship, it is highly probable that sooner or later personal material will surface. We are all of us vulnerable in this way, as there are bound to be issues that affect us personally, sometimes with their origins buried in our past. Often the first indication we have is when we find ourselves behaving unusually or unpredictably with our group, perhaps talking too much, or heatedly, or even verbally attacking or strongly disagreeing with a member. One of the purposes of review is to enable the leader to chart any such areas that are especially tender, and to work out ways of coping with them when they arise, so that the group is not impeded in its work.

Figure 25 Verbally attacking a member

Just how far this process should go is debatable. It could happen that a leader becomes so interested in individual personal material with the consultant that the group is lost sight of altogether. If this happens, it means that the personal therapy of the leader is being promoted, and the proper conduct of the group neglected. Both are important. It can be convincingly argued that, in the interests of clarity, they should be conducted separately with different people, and ideally perhaps they should. Realistically, however, there may not be too many alternatives available, especially if you live far from large conurbations. Rather than saying categorically that you should not use your group consultant supervisor for personal therapy but purely to focus on the group, we would say it is vital to discuss such issues between you, and know when you are doing which. It would then be vital to be watchful not to neglect contemplation of your group and your part in it. Although the leader's personal therapy cannot be the prime aim in running a support group for others, properly conducted supervision can nevertheless instigate therapeutic insights relevant to the leader and so be personally helpful.

From time to time, a personal issue will surface which is too complex and demanding to be accommodated within supervision. At such times it is highly recommended that an individual therapist be found, who can concentrate on the leader's own personal material. This has proved necessary when leaders have realized they're being deeply personally affected by, for example, such issues as loss, abandonment, neglect, despair, and all kinds of abuse.

Agreeing a contract

Perhaps at this point we can introduce the idea of a 'contract' between supervisor and supervisee. Such a contract may indeed be an actual piece of paper, and fairly formally constituted but it may well be sufficient to have made a verbal agreement between supervisor and supervisee (and also line management if the supervision is being paid for by an agency). Below, we give an example of such a contract. It is very loosely based on an actual working contract for professionals, which was developed originally by the Freshfields Drugs Agency in Truro, Cornwall, after consultation between line management, external supervisors, counsellors and other front-line workers. Freshfields is a non-statutory charitable organization set up to provide counselling and other services to street drug-users, and aims to deliver the highest professional counselling and support services to clients, while working in association with county-wide medical and other official agencies. In 2003 it was the first company in the country to be accorded the status of 'Accredited Service' by the British Association for Counselling and Psychotherapy, which means that while working within the agency, all the counsellors are working to accredited and approved professional standards.

Case study Supervision contract

Aspects of the non-managerial supervision contract and guide

1   We look at any issues you consider important.

2   Is anything about the group stressing you? If so, what do you think is causing it? Can you think of anything that might be done to help? Have you tried anything already? Is that working? What do you need to do next? Is there anything in the way?

3   How effective are you feeling – what is working well? Are you getting any feedback (from colleagues, your group, from other professionals)?

4   Are there any individual exchanges in the group that you're wondering about?

5   Is your work with your group having any effect on you outside the group time? If so, does anything need to be done about that?

6   How are you feeling right now about this process and this supervision?

Not all aspects need to be covered at every meeting.

Confidentiality

- Supervision is a confidential relationship with the following limitation: Should a situation occur in which the supervisor feels that the worker's own well-being or the well-being of group members is at risk, the supervisor should bring this up with the supervisee. An agreement needs to be jointly reached as to what further action, if any, the supervisor should undertake.

- Supervision aims to be a safe relationship for both participants.

- Agreement needs to be reached as to how often supervision should take place.

- It is recommended that the worker and supervisor review supervision at least every three years.

It can be seen that even drastically slimmed down from the professional contract, such an agreement establishes a solid framework for exploration and productive discussion, ensuring that the main bases are covered, without being too prescriptive and authoritarian.

Not all contracts need be quite so detailed, as long as both supervisee and supervisor are agreed on the form of the work, and are clear about how it should progress. The contract above does give some idea of the ground it might be useful to consider before starting work together. It does need to be understood that the final responsibility for how the leader might behave in the group lies with the leader, not the supervisor, for in the end it is the leader who is in the 'hot seat', having to deal with the consequences of their interventions there and then, in the group as things happen, and perhaps later if things have gone wrong and there are complaints to be answered. Mercifully, if the group has been reasonably well run, such a turn of events is unlikely, even very unlikely. However, both supervisor and supervisee remain at all times accountable for their conduct, and should be prepared to explain their actions if so required under appropriate circumstances, notably to their respective professional bodies, if they have them.

The frequency of supervision

It is generally a good idea to develop a regular habit of supervision, as it is sometimes surprising how time can fly by without a leader's closely examining the group's progress. If all is well, perhaps it may be possible to 'get away with it' for a while but in the group's life small events left unattended can quickly become big issues. If the leader has not noticed their development, it can come as quite a surprise when something blows up 'out of the blue', when really the warning signs have been present for some time. Ideally, then, the worker should be looking to establish regular sessions with their consultant, at an interval not too widely spaced, once a month, say, if their group is running weekly, at a time which is convenient to both, and properly negotiated. Certainly, it is most advisable to be on the look-out for behavioural clues that the group is beginning to acquire a disproportionate importance in your life. Such indicators would include disturbed sleep patterns, e.g. lying awake thinking about the group, or issues that have been raised during session, dreams about the group or its members, and so on. If you detect such signs, you really need to take this to supervision without delay.

A second area needing prompt attention is if you find yourself becoming fixated on an individual in the group, or their personal issues.

Case study   Dangers of lack of supervision

The staff members of a residential institution caring for very disturbed young people were each receiving personal individual supervision from the same external consultant. There came a point at which the consultant was dramatically dismissed on the spot when it became apparent that he had been conducting one affair after another with his female supervisees. Interestingly, they did not complain about his conduct as such, remarkably taking the view that, 'We're all over 21, so fair enough.' They were, however, all outraged when he started discussing one conquest with another, feeling totally betrayed, and so his activities came to light. The whole sorry saga was nevertheless contained within a whole staff support group run by a different external supervisor, where some processing of the emotions was possible, and total disaster was avoided. This staff group had been established over time by regular meetings, and proved its worth in salvaging something from the crisis.

There are two noteworthy aspects to this story:

1   The staff support group was severely tested, but survived, facilitating the processing of very difficult emotional material, enabling the staff to continue with their difficult work.

> 2   If the erring supervisor had himself taken appropriate care to have his own work properly supervised, a great deal of anguish and professional damage could and should have been avoided.

By now we hope the reader has a clearer picture of how we see good supervision being conducted, and some of its benefits. It is a common experience for supervisees to arrive somewhat troubled, without quite being able to say precisely why, but feeling blocked and unclear about how to move forward, and often tired out. After a good supervision session, after a further hour or so of really quite searching hard work, instead of feeling even more exhausted, it's not unusual to feel refreshed, having found a new sense of direction and encouragement. Even though no direct advice as such may have been given, no 'medicine' for the ailing leader prescribed, somehow the spirit has been lifted. Good supervision may then produce an effect not too dissimilar to the effects we look for in a well-run support group. It is a good investment of time for a support group leader.

Finale

In writing this book, we have attempted to produce a 'first reader' for a practitioner, generic in nature and drawing on wide theoretical bases. If you do decide to run a support group, we would hope that early encounters with your group will be successful, and that you will thus feel encouraged to continue the search for resources to assist you in developing competence and effectiveness. If you are really fortunate, you may be able to find, or set up, a group for group leaders, where the work is primarily focused on leading groups, and on supporting and developing members in that role. As an example, the Balint Society runs a group leaders' workshop for leaders of Balint Groups. These groups are aimed at encouraging and enabling doctors to consider the nature and potency of the doctor–patient relationship. Originally designed for doctors, in recent years an enlightened approach has seen this type of group opened to other skilled leaders such as nurses, psychotherapists, and counsellors. The workshop is held from time to time, usually in London at the Royal College of General Practice. Each session is devoted to the work of one of the members, as evidenced by a transcript of a recent group they have run. The transcript is circulated before the meeting, thus giving everyone time to consider it in detail before the workshop. The overall idea is not too dissimilar from our very first example, the pain clinic, where the exchange of genuine feeling, the look in the psychological mirror, the generation of new possibilities, ideas, and ways of being, all serve both to support and challenge the members as group leaders. Another ready and regular resource is the monthly articles that appear in the 'Group-work' and

'Supervision' sections of the *Counselling and Psychotherapy Journal* published by the British Association for Counselling and Psychotherapy.

We hope that it is clear that the approach to evaluation that we have outlined in itself constitutes a recipe for the continuing development of oneself as a leader. In a very real sense, the work of development is never-ending – there is no point at which one can rest and say, 'There, now I'm fully trained, and need not do any more training.' The process is ongoing, and consists of modifying practice as a result of sober, careful, and extensive considerations of experience, and doing no harm in the meantime. The key factor is not so much the piling up of many hours of experience, nor even the acquisition of certificates and diplomas, but the seeking of informed, reliable and accurate feedback as to effective practice. Given a commitment to the processes and practices we have described throughout the volume, there should be a steady maturation of the beginner to a competent group leader.

The process is somewhat similar to learning to drive a car. We have aimed this book at relatively inexperienced colleagues contemplating their first group, that is, with their 'L' plates on. The whole point of the driving test is not to certify everyone passing as fully competent, but that they are safe to go out on the road and begin the process of learning to become a good driver. For group leaders there is no driving test, but we are confident that if the ways we have recommended of going about things are followed, then it should be

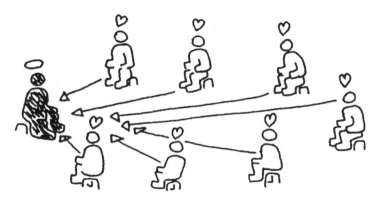

Figure 26 The leader may find a true sense of worth

comparatively safe to start work on becoming a good group leader. We hope that you will experience the great sense of worth and personal satisfaction which comes from leading a successful support group.

References

Alexander, P. (2004) Psychology and palliative care, *Clinical Psychology*, 43: 40–3.

Aranda, S. (2004) The cost of caring, in S. Payne, J. Seymour and L. Ingleton (eds) *Palliative Care Nursing*. Maidenhead: Open University Press.

Aveline, M. and Dryden, W. (1988) *Group Therapy in Britain*. Milton Keynes: Open University Press.

Bailey, R. D. (1985) *Coping with Stress in Caring*. Oxford: Blackwell.

Barraclough, J. (1994) *Cancer and Emotion*. Chichester: John Wiley & Sons, Ltd.

Baum, A., Newman, S., Weinman, J., West R. and McManus, C. (1997) *Cambridge Handbook of Psychology, Health and Medicine*. Cambridge: University Press Cambridge.

Bennett, P. and Connell, H. (1988) Couples coping with myocardial infarction: the partner's experience, *Coronary Health Care*, 2(3); 140–4.

Berne, E. (1964) *Games People Play: The Psychology of Human Relationships*. New York: Grove Press.

Berne, E. (1966) *Principles of Group Treatment*. New York: Oxford University Press.

Berne, E. (1972) *What Do You Say After You Say Hello?* London: Corgi.

Bion, W. R. (1961) *Experiences in Groups*. London: Tavistock.

Briggs, K. and Askham, J. (1999) *The Needs of People with Dementia and Those Who Care for Them: A Review of the Literature*. London: Alzheimer's Society.

British Association for Counselling and Psychotherapy (2002) *Ethical Framework for Good Practice in Counselling and Psychotherapy*. Rugby: British Association for Counselling and Psychotherapy.

Brown, A. (1986) *Group Work*. Aldershot: Gower.

Brown, G. W. and Harris, T. O. (1978) *Social Origins of Depression*. London: Tavistock.

Cartwright, S and Cooper, C. L. (1997) *Managing Workplace Stress*. London: Sage.

Cherniss, C. (1980) *Staff Burn-out: Job Stress in the Human Services*. Newbury Park, CA: Sage.

Cole, M. and Walker, S. (1989) *Teaching and Stress*. Milton Keynes: Open University Press.

Cox, M. (1978) *Structuring the Therapeutic Process*. Oxford: Pergamon.

Dryden, W. (1985) *Therapists' Dilemmas*. London: Harper & Row.

Dryden, W. and Thorne, B. (eds) (1991) *Training and Supervision for Counselling in Action*. London: Sage.

Finlay, L. (1993) *Groupwork in Occupational Therapy*. Cheltenham: Nelson Thornes.

Firth-Cozens, J. (1987) Emotional distress in junior house officers, *British Medical Journal*, 295: 533–6.

Freudenberger, H. J. (1974) Staff burn-out, *Journal of Social Issues*, 30: 159–65.

Ganster, D. C. and Victor, B. (1988) The impact of social support on mental and physical health, *British Journal of Medical Psychology*, 61: 17–36.

Gendlin, E. T. (1978) *Focusing*. New York: Everest House.

Gillibrand, R. (2004) What differentiates the young person with diabetes exhibiting good metabolic control and poor metabolic control? A qualitative analysis, *Psychology Health Update*, 13: 18–20.

Hall, L. and Lloyd, S. (1993) *Surviving Child Sexual Abuse*. London: The Falmer Press.

Halpen, D. (2005) *Social Capital*. Cambridge: Polity Press.

Hossack, A. and Wall, G. (2005) Service users: undervalued and underused, *The Psychologist*, 18: 134–6.

Hyde, K. (1988) Analytic group psychotherapies, in N. Aveline and W. Dryden (eds) *Group Therapy in Britain*. Milton Keynes: Open University Press.

Jenkinson, J. D. and Smerdon, G. (1988) A final year trainee group, *Journal of the Association of Course Organisers*, 4: 16–22.

Johnston, N. (1985) Occupational stress and the professional pilot; the role of the pilot advisory group (PAG), *Aviation, Space, and Environmental Medicine*, July, 633–7.

Joseph, S., Williams, R. and Yule, W. (1997) *Understanding Post-Traumatic Stress*. Chichester: John Wiley & Sons, Ltd.

Kelly, G. A. (1955) *The Psychology of Personal Constructs*, vols 1 and 2. New York: W.W. Norton.

Kennedy, S., Kiecolt-Glaser, J. K. and Glaser, R. (1988) Immunological consequences of acute and chronic stressors: mediating role of interpersonal relationships, *British Journal of Medical Psychology*, 61: 77–85.

Lakin, M. (1985) *The Helping Group: Therapeutic Principles and Issues*. Reading, MA: Addison-Wesley.

Lane, D., Carroll, D. and Ring, C. (2002) The prevalence and persistence of depression and anxiety following myocardial infarction, *British Journal of Health Psychology*, 7: 11–21.

Lawton, B. (2000) Rethinking supervision, *Counselling*, 11: 486–7.

Llewelyn, S. and Payne, S. (1995) Caring: the cost to nurses and families, in A. Broome and S. Llewelyn (eds) *Health Psychology*. London: Chapman and Hall.

Martin, P. (1997) *The Sickening Mind: Brain, Behaviour, Immunity and Disease*. London: HarperCollins.

Marx, J. A. and Gelso, C. J. (1987) Termination of individual counseling in a university counseling center, *Journal of Counseling Psychology*, 34: 3–9.

Miller, P. M. and Ingham, J. G. (1976) Friends, confidants and symptoms, *Social Psychiatry*, 11: 51–8.

Nichols, K. A. (1976) Preparation for membership in a group, *Bulletin of the British Psychological Society*, 29: 353–9.

Nichols, K. A. (1987) Teaching nurses psychological care, in D. Muller (ed.) *Teaching Psychological Skills to Nurses*. Leicester: British Psychological Society.

Nichols, K. A. (2003) *Psychological Care for Ill and Injured People*. Maidenhead: Open University Press.

Nichols, K. A. (2004) Psychological care in palliative care. Address given at the annual conference of the Catalan Palliative Care Association, Barcelona.

Ogden, J. (2004) *Health Psychology*. Maidenhead: Open University Press.

Olohan, S. (2004) Student mental health – a university challenge? *The Psychologist*, 17: 192–5.

Patterson, C. H. (1986) *Theories of Counselling and Psychotherapy*. New York: Harper and Row.

Payne, R. and Firth-Cozens, J. (1987) *Stress in Health Professionals*. Chichester: John Wiley & Sons, Ltd.

Payne, S. and Haines, R. (2002) Doing our bit to ease the pain, *The Psychologist*, 15: 564–7.

Payne, S., Seymour, J. and Ingleton, I. (2004) *Palliative Care Nursing*. Maidenhead. Open University Press.

Pratchett, T. (1989) *Pyramids*. London: Victor Gollancz.

Quigney, C. and Callaghan, W. (2005) Participants' views on a Pain Management Programme: a qualitative analysis, *Health Psychology Update*, 14: 14–21.

Raphael, B. (1986) *When Disaster Strikes: A Handbook for the Caring Professions*. London: Hutchinson.

Rawle, H., Hunter, M. S. and Westlake, A. (2005) Developing clinical health psychology services for people attending cardiac rehabilitation, *Clinical Psychology*, 48: 12–16.

Rogers, C. R. (1961) *On Becoming a Person: A Therapist's View of Psychotherapy*. Boston: Houghton Mifflin.

Skirrow, P., Jones, C., Griffiths, R. D. and Kaney, S. (2001) Intensive care: easing the trauma, *The Psychologist*, 14: 640–2.

Whitaker, D. S. (1985) *Using Groups to Help People*. London: Tavistock/Routledge.

Whitaker, D. S. and Lieberman, M. A. (1964) *Psychotherapy through the Group Process*. New York: Atherton Press.

Williams, R. B., Barefoot, J. C. and Califf, R. M. (1992) Prognostic importance of social resources among patients with CAD, *Journal of the American Medical Association*, 267: 520–4.

Yalom, I. D. (1985) *The Theory and Practice of Group Psychotherapy*. New York: Basic Books.

Yaskowich, K. M. and Stam, H. J. (2003) Cancer narratives and the Cancer Support Group, *Journal of Health Psychology*, 8: 720–37.

Useful addresses

British Association for Counselling and Psychotherapy,
BACP House,
35–37 Albert St,
Rugby, Warwickshire CV21 2SG.

The British Psychological Society,
St Andrews House,
48 Princess Road East,
Leicester LE1 7DR

The Freshfield Service Ltd,
Lander House,
5, Upper Lemon Villas,
Truro TR1 2PD,
(tel.) 01872 241952.

The Balint Society,
www.balint.co.uk,
Dr. David Watt,
Hon. Sec.,
220 Tollgate Road,
London E6 4JS,
(tel.) 020 7474 5656.

Index

Page numbers for figures have suffix **f**